COLLINS GEM

BABIES NAMES

Revised edition prepared
by Julia Cresswell

D0267436

HarperCollins Publishers
P. O. Box, Glasgow G4 0NB

First published as *Collins Gem Dictionary of First Names* 1967
Second edition published as *Collins Gem First Names* 1988
First published as *Collins Gem Babies Names* 1992
Third edition 1993

Reprint 9 8 7 6 5 4 3

ISBN 0 00 470116 X

Printed in Great Britain by
HarperCollins Manufacturing, Glasgow

Contents

Introduction

This little book is designed to help you choose a name for your baby. Even parents who know what they want to call their child may well want to look at some of the possible forms the name can take, and find out something about its history and meaning. To this end, I have crammed in as many names and variants as possible. Variations in the forms of names have all been cross-referenced, unless they would fall next to the entry in which they are to be found. So if you cannot find the name you want in this book, look for the nearest spelling and read the entry there.

Today's parents have a much wider choice of names than their grandparents did. We have adopted a large number of foreign names, use an ever-increasing number of surnames as first names, and freely invent names or create blends, joining parts of different names to make a new name. But if you look at the lists of most popular names in this book, you will see that all of them have been around for hundreds of years and the majority of names still come from the Bible, from classical literature or are developments of the names used by our ancestors. These old names come from two main language groups. The Celtic names, which can be from Welsh (or the British language it comes from); from Irish Gaelic, described as 'Irish'; or from Scots Gaelic, for which 'Gaelic' is used. Occasionally we do not know which of the languages they come from, or they are shared by the Scots and Irish, in which case 'Celtic' is used. To save space many of these Celtic names have been put under English names which were used as substitutes in the bad old days when an ethnic name was not acceptable in certain areas of life. The other group of names is described as 'Old German'. Some of these were used by the Anglo-Saxon inhabitants of Britain, who spoke a Germanic dialect called Old English. Many were brought over by the Normans, who, although they spoke French, were descendants of Vikings and not only used their own Germanic names, but had also adopted the Old German names used by the French nobility, themselves descended from other Germanic invaders.

The first edition of this book was compiled in 1967 by Sandra Bance BA Hons, Mary Laird and Charles Wacher, under the supervision of Mr A.G. Hepburn ALA, former Head Librarian of the Mitchell Library, Glasgow, and Mr R. E. Adams

BA ALA, of the National Library of Scotland, Edinburgh. Since then I have twice revised it, to bring it up to date with current trends in naming and with modern studies of names. Advice on Irish names has been given by Nicole Müller, but any errors remain my own. A guide to the anglicized pronunciation of some of the Irish names has been given, but no attempt has been made to show the true Irish pronunciation. Help has also been given with the usual pronunciation of other names where it is not immediately apparent. Where a re-spelling of a name shows how it is pronounced, it is described as a 'phonetic spelling'.

Julia Cresswell
1993

Registering your baby's birth

If you have your baby in a hospital in England or Wales, there is a good chance that your local registrar's office will have a branch there. It is worth taking advantage of this facility, rather than having to cope with a new baby and getting down to the registrar's office later on. If nothing is said at the hospital, ask one of the nurses. Unfortunately, this facility is not available in Scotland where the regulations concerning the registration of births vary slightly from those in England and Wales.

By law, you have to register the birth of your child within 42 days of his or her birth, or within 21 days in Scotland. If you have not used a hospital office, you can go to any registrar's office, although the procedure is slightly simpler if you use your local one, the address of which should be in the phone book. Registration centres round the mother. If the baby's parents are married either parent can register the birth. If they are not married, they can register the birth together if they go to the registrar together, or else the father must get special forms from the registrar's office in advance which, when filled in, will enable his details to go on the birth certificate. Otherwise, the father's details will be left blank, although it may be possible to fill these in later — talk to the registrar about this. There is no need to take the baby with you to the registrar, but only a parent can register the birth; a friend or relative will not do.

At the registrar's you will be asked to give the following information. The place and date of the baby's birth (the time of birth will only be needed if you have twins or more, although in Scotland it is always required). You will also need to state its sex, and will be asked for the names you intend to give it. If the father's details are to go on the form you will need to give his full name, his date and place of birth and his occupation. The mother will be asked to give her full name, her maiden name if she has changed her surname and her place and date of birth. If she wishes, an occupation (current or previous) can be filled in. She has to give her usual address at the time of the birth and, if she is married to the father, the date of marriage will be asked for. She will also be asked for the number of other children she has had.

All this information will be entered into a register, which you should then check carefully — it will be difficult to correct mistakes later — and then sign. You will then be given a free short birth certificate which is all you need. You can also get full copies of the information on the register if you would like to have them, and spare copies of either type of certificate. In England and Wales, the cost of a full certificate is currently £2.50, of additional short ones £1.50 if you get them at the time of registration; later they cost £2.50 and £5.50. In Scotland, the full certificate costs £5.50, as do additional short ones bought up to one month after the date of registration after which the cost rises. It is probably worth considering an extra copy so that each parent can have one, or so that one can be sent off with something like an application for a passport and you can still have one to hand.

If you still have not decided on a name for your baby by the time the limit for registration is up, you must still register the birth, but the name can be left blank. You then have up to one year from registration to make up your minds, although in Scotland any correction to the records after registration is likley to attract a fee. If your baby is baptised, the baptismal certificate can be produced at the registrar's office as evidence of the child's name. (Extra names given at baptism can also be added in this way.) Otherwise you need to ask the registrar's office for a Certificate of Naming, and use this to have the names inserted. You can give your child any forenames or surname that you like. In Scotland the registrar has the power to refuse to record a name if he or she deems it to be potentially offensive, although in practice a name is rarely objected to. In England and Wales, the registrar has no right to refuse your choice, although if your choice is too outrageous you may find that you are asked to think of the effect on the child before confirming it is what you want. Modern registrars are trained to be friendly and helpful, and you can always phone your local office for any advice you need; alternatively, contact The General Register Office, Smedley Hydro, Trafalgar Road, Birkdale, Southport PR8 2HH (tel. 0704-69824) or The Registrar General's Office for Scotland, New Register House, Edinburgh (tel. 031-334 0380).

A

Aaron *m.*
In the Old Testament, Aaron was the brother of
Moses and the first High Priest of Israel. The
name has traditionally been interpreted as from
the Hebrew for 'high mountain', but like Moses,
Aaron is probably an Egyptian name of
unknown meaning. It is connected with the
Arabic names *Harun* and *Haroun*, and has been
in use since the Reformation. It has recently
become more popular, particularly in the USA.

Abagail, Abb(e)y, Abbie *see* **Abigail**

Abby *see* **Gabriel**

Abe, Abie *see* **Abel, Abraham**

Abel *m.*
In the Old Testament, Abel was the second son

of **Adam** and **Eve** and murdered by his brother Cain. The name may come from a Hebrew word meaning 'breath', but like so many of the earliest names, its meaning is rather doubtful. The name has been in use in England since before the Norman Conquest. The short forms include *Abe* and *Abie*.

Abigail *f.*

From the Hebrew, meaning 'father rejoiced'. It was the name of one of King David's wives and was much used in England during the 16th and 17th centuries when many Old Testament names were popular. It was so popular for working-class women that it degenerated into a term for a lady's maid and so became unfashionable; but is now coming back into fashion. It is sometimes spelt *Abagail*, or *Abigal*. The short forms include *Abbie*, *Abbey*, *Abby* (also used for **Gabrielle**) and **Gail**.

Abner *m.*

From the Hebrew words for 'father of light'. In the Bible it is the name of King Saul's cousin, who was commander of the army. In England it came into common use, together with other biblical names, after the Reformation in the early 16th century. It is still found occasionally in North America.

Abraham *m.*

This is the name of the Old Testament patriarch who, for the first 90 years of his life, was called *Abram*, 'high father', but then was told by God that he should be called Abraham, 'father of many nations'. It was used in England regularly after the Reformation and became popular in North America where the abbreviation *Abe*, as in President Abe Lincoln (1809-65), was widely used. Other short forms are *Abie, Ham* and *Bram*.

Absalom *see* Axel

Ada *m.*

A name which started life as a pet form for **Adela**, **Adelaide** and **Adeline**, and so means 'noble'. It was fashionable in Britain in the late 18th and 19th centuries, but is now rare. *Adah* is often confused with Ada, but is in fact derived from the Hebrew word for 'ornament' or 'brightness' and occurs in the Old Testament Book of Genesis. Popular in England in the 19th century, it is still used occasionally in North America.

Adam *m.*

From the Hebrew, meaning 'red', possibly referring either to skin colour, or to the clay from
which God formed the first man. The name was
adopted by the Irish as early as the 7th century,
when St *Adamnan*, 'Little Adam', was Abbot of
Iona. It was very common in the 13th century
and has been in use ever since, particularly in
Scotland. It is currently one of the more popular
boys' names. *Adamina* is a rare feminine form.

Adela *f.*

From the Old German, meaning 'noble'. It was
common among the Normans, who brought it to
England. One of William the Conqueror's
daughters had this name. It died out but was
later revived and became fashionable in the
French form *Adèle*. *Addie* or *Addy* are used as a
pet form for each of the names derived from this
root (see below). Adela can also be spelt *Adella*,
which gives us the name **Della**, now more
popular than its source.

Adelaide *f.*

Derived from the Old German words meaning
'noble and kind'. It was common for centuries

on the Continent but only came to Britain in 1830 when Adelaide of Saxe-Coburg became queen. Adelaide, capital city of South Australia, was named after this popular queen. **Ada** is sometimes used as a pet form (see also **Alida**, **Heidi**).

Adèle *see* **Adela**

Adelice, Adelise *see* **Alice**

Adeline *f.*
Like **Adelaide** this name is derived from the Old German for 'noble'. It was first cited in England in the Domesday Book, and was common during the Middle Ages. After that it disappeared until the Victorian Gothic revival. It is best known from the song *Sweet Adeline*. **Ada** is sometimes used as a pet form and *Aline*, now used as a separate name was also once a short form.

Adella *see* **Adela**

Adolph
Although Adolph ('noble wolf') and the Latinized form of the name, **Adolphus**, have

never been common names in this country, and
received a further set-back with the rise of
Adolph Hitler, the short forms *Dolph* and
Dolphus are sometimes found.

Adrian *m.*, Adrienne *f.*

From the Latin, meaning 'man from Adria', and
a form of the name of the Roman Emperor
Hadrian, who built the wall across northern
England. It has been used since Roman times; a
St Adrian was martyred in the 4th century and
another helped organize the English Church in
the 7th century. *Adriana* is a rare female form,
the French Adrienne being more popular today.
Adria and *Adrianne* are also found.

Aeneas *m.*

The name of the legendary hero of Virgil's
Aeneid, who is said to have escaped from the
sack of Troy to Italy and laid the foundations of
the civilization of Rome. The name has been
used in Britain since the Renaissance, most
frequently in Scotland where it is used as a form
of the Gaelic *Aonghas* (see **Angus**).

Aengus *see* Angus

Afra *see* **Aphra**

Agatha *f.*

From the Greek meaning 'good woman', was the name of a 3rd-century martyr and saint. The name has been out of fashion for some years, but shows slight signs of a revival. The short form is *Aggie*.

Agnes *f.*

From the Greek meaning 'pure'. There was an early Christian martyr called Agnes, whose symbol is a lamb, since the name also sounds very like the Latin *agnus*, 'lamb'. Old forms still occasionally used include *Annis, Annice* and *Annes*. *Agneta* is the Swedish form and *Inez* is the anglicized form of the Spanish *Inés*. Agnes was popular in Scotland where it also became *Nessie* and *Nessa*. In Wales it became *Nest* and *Nesta*. *Aggie* is a short form shared with **Agatha** (see also **Ina**).

Aidan *m.*

An ancient Irish name meaning 'little fire'. It was the name of a 7th-century Irish missionary who founded the monastery of Lindisfarne in Northumbria. It was revived during the 19th century and is popular at the moment in Ireland. It is sometimes anglicised as *Edan*. *Hayden* (*Haydon*, *Hadyn*) is said to be a Welsh form of the name.

Ailbhe *see* **Elvis**

Aileen *see* **Eileen**

Ailis, Ailish *see* **Alice**

Ailsa *f.*
From the name of the Scottish island, Ailsa Craig. First used in Scotland, where it can also be a pet form of **Alice**, it has now spread to the rest of the country.

Aimée *see* **Amy, Esmé**

Ainsley *m. and f.*
A place and surname used as a first name, this comes from the Old English and probably means 'lonely clearing'. It is also spelt *Ainslie*.

Aisha *see* **Ayesha**

Aisling *f.*
The commonest form of a name also found as

Aislinn, *Isleen* and the phonetic *Ashling*. It is an old Irish name meaning 'a dream, vision' and has been rather popular in Ireland since the 1960s.

Aithne *see* Eithne

Al *see* Alastair, Alexander

Alan m.

An old Celtic name of unknown meaning. It has appeared in various forms from early times. In England it first became popular after the Norman Conquest as *Alain* or *Alein*, the French forms. These developed into Alleyne which is preserved as a surname. Alan, *Allan*, *Allen* and *Alun* (strictly speaking, a Welsh river name used as a first name) are in use today. *Alana*, the feminine form, is also spelt *Allana*, *Alanah* and *Alanna*. The actress *Lana* Turner made the short form well known.

Alastair m.

Also spelt **Alasdair**, **Alistair** and **Alister,** this is the Gaelic form of **Alexander**, 'defender of men'. It is shortened to *Al*, *Ali*, *Alli* or *Ally*, *Alec* and *Alick*.

Alban *m.*

From the Latin *Albanus*, meaning 'man from Alba' (a Roman town whose name means 'white'), and the name of the earliest British saint. The town of St Albans, where he was martyred, is named after him. The name was never common, but it was revived under the influence of the Oxford Movement in the 19th century. *Albin* and *Albinus* are variants which appear occasionally (see also **Albinia**).

Alberic *see* Aubrey

Albert *m.*

An Old German name meaning 'noble and bright'. The Old English form was *Ethelbert*, the name of the Kentish king who welcomed Augustine to Canterbury when he came to convert the Anglo-Saxons to Christianity. This was replaced after the Norman Conquest by the French form, Aubert. Albert became so popular after the marriage of Queen Victoria to Prince Albert of Saxe-Coburg that it became over-used and so went out of fashion. **Bert** and **Bertie** are short forms. *Alberta*, *Albertina* and *Albertine* are forms of the name used for girls.

Albin, Albinus *see* **Alban**

Albinia *f.*
Also spelt *Albina*, this name comes from the Latin meaning 'white' and is thus the female equivalent of **Alban**. It was often used in the 17th and 18th centuries, but is now uncommon

Alby *see* **Elvis**

Aldous *m.*
is from the Old German Aldo, meaning 'old'. It has been used in the eastern counties of England since the 13th century and has given rise to various surnames like Aldhouse and Aldiss. *Aldo* is still used in North America. The writer Aldous Huxley (1894-1963) is the best-known British example.

Alec *see* **Alastair, Alexander**

Aled *m.*
is the name of a Welsh river used as a first name. There is a female form **Aledwen**, 'fair Aled'.

Alein *see* **Alan**

Alessandra *see* **Sandra**

Alethea *f.*
From the Greek word meaning 'truth'. It was
much used in the 17th century in England.
Variant forms include *Alethia* and *Aletia*.

Alex *see* **Alexander**

Alexa *see* **Alexis**

Alexander *m.*
Currently one of the most popular boy's names,
this comes from the Greek meaning 'defender of
men'. It was made famous in the 4th century BC
by Alexander the Great, and was very popular in
England in the Middle Ages. *Sandy* is a pet
form, particularly in Scotland. *Alex* is the most
common of the many short forms, others being
Al, *Alec*, *Ali*, *Lex*, *Xan* and *Xander*. **Sacha** is
another form of the name.

Alexandra *f.*
The feminine form of **Alexander**, and like it,
currently popular. **Sandra** was originally an
Italian form, but has become established as a
name in its own right. It shares pet and short

forms with **Alexander**, while *Alix* or *Alyx* can be a form of this name or of **Alice**. *Alexandria* and *Alexandrina* are also found.

Alexis *m. and f.*

From the Greek word meaning 'helper' or 'defender' and is the name of one of the great saints of the Orthodox church. Originally a man's name, it is now more frequently used for women. *Alexie* is an alternative form for boys, and *Alexia* and *Alexa* for girls.

Alfred *m.*

From two Old English words, meaning 'elf' (hence 'good') and 'counsel'. It is also a possible development of the Anglo-Saxon name Ealdfrith, meaning 'old peace'. It is sometimes written *Alfrid*. When Alfred was written down in old Latin, the name was spelt *Alured* and developed into Avery, which survives as a surname. The original Alfred was re-introduced in the 18th century and became very popular in the 19th and earlier 20th centuries which led to a decline in use later on. *Alf, Alfie* and *Fred* are diminutives. There is a feminine form *Alfreda*, and *Elfrida*, although it technically comes from a slightly different name meaning 'elf-strength', is probably also used as a female version of Alfred.

Algernon *m.*

From a Norman French nickname meaning 'with whiskers'. It was popular in the 19th century but is not much used today. The usual diminutive is *Algie* or *Algy*.

Ali *see* Alastair, Alexander, Alice

Alia *see* Ella

Alice *f.*

From the Old German word for 'nobility'. It originally had the form *Adelice* or *Adelise*. A number of forms remained popular from the Middle Ages until the 17th century, when it went out of favour. It was revived again in the 19th century together with the variant *Alicia*. Nowadays these have developed additional forms such as *Allice, Allyce* and *Alyssa, Alisa, Alissa*. *Alison* is a variant. *Alys* is the Welsh form and Irish forms are *Alis, Ailis* or the phonetic *Ailish*. *Ali, Allie* and *Alley* are used as pet forms, while *Alix* and *Alyx* can be used either as forms of Alice or **Alexandra**.

Alick *see* **Alastair**

Alida *f.*
A Hungarian pet form of **Adelaide**, 'noble and kind', which is sometimes found in this country.

Aline *see* **Adeline**

Alis, Alisa *see* **Alice**

Alison *f.*
Originally a diminutive of **Alice** that was adopted in the 13th century, but which was soon treated as a separate name. It was at one time a particularly Scottish name. Pet forms include those used for **Alice** and **Elsie** and it can be found in the forms *Alyson* and *Allyson*.

Alissa *see* **Alice**

Alistair, Alister *see* **Alastair**

Alix *see* **Alexandra, Alice**

Allan, Allana, Allen *see* **Alan**

Allegra *f.*
An Italian word meaning 'cheerful, lively', given

by the poet Lord Byron to his daughter and still used occasionally as a result.

Alley *see* **Alice**

Alli, Ally, *see* **Alastair**

Allice, Allie, Allyce *see* **Alice, Alison**

Alma *f.*
There are many opinions about the derivation of this name. It can be explained as from the Hebrew word for 'maiden', the Latin for 'kind' or the Italian for 'soul'. Most importantly, the name became very popular after the Battle of Alma during the Crimean War, and is still found occasionally.

Aloysius *m.*
This is the Latin form of *Aloys*, an old Provençal form of **Louis**. There was a popular Spanish saint of this name in the 16th century and Roman Catholics continue to use the name in this country. *Aloys* or *Aloyse* was the female form of the old name, and is a possible source of **Eloise**.

Althea *f.*
From the Greek for 'wholesome', and was the
Greek name for the marsh mallow plant, still
used as a healing herb. It appears to have been
introduced to England with various other
classical names during the Stuart period, and
appeared in the charming lyric by Richard
Lovelace *To Althea from Prison.*

Alun *see* **Alan**

Alured *see* **Alfred**

Alvin *m.*
From two Old English names, Alwine, meaning
'friend of all' and Athelwine 'noble friend'. It is
not very common in Britain, but is found fairly
frequently in North America. *Aylwin* is an
alternative form of the name, as are *Alvan* and
Alvyn. There is a rare feminine *Alvina*. The
similar-sounding *Alvar* means 'elf army'.

Alys, Alyssa *see* **Alice**

Alyson, Alysson *see* **Alison**

Alyx *see* **Alexandra, Alice**

Amabel *f.*

From the Latin for 'lovable'. It had been in use
in England in various forms since the 12th
century. The short form, **Mabel**, early became
established as an independent name.

Amanda *f.*

From the Latin meaning 'deserving love'. It
appears first in Restoration plays, where many
classical or pseudo-classical names were introduced or fabricated. It has remained in use since
then and is still popular. *Mandy* is a pet form
also used as a name in its own right.

Amaryllis *f.*

Originally from Greek, probably meaning
'sparkling', and used by Greek poets as a name
for a country girl. It served the same purpose for
Latin poets, and was introduced to Britain via
English poetry in the 17th century.

Amalia *see* Amelia

Amata *see* Amy

Amber *f.*

The name of the gemstone, used as a first

name. It was not used before this century but has gained in popularity recently.

Ambrose *m.*

From the Greek for 'divine'. There was a 4th-century St Ambrose who was Bishop of Milan. The name is found in the Domesday Book and has been used occasionally ever since. The Welsh name *Emrys* is derived from the Latin form of the name. There is a rare feminine form, *Ambrosine*.

Amelia *f.*

From an Old German name possibly meaning 'work', its form is perhaps influenced by *Emilia* (see **Emily**). The rarer *Amalia* is another form of the name. It can be shortened to *Milly*.

Aminta *see* **Araminta**

Amos *m.*

A Hebrew name, possibly meaning 'he who carries a burden'. It was the name of an Old Testament prophet and was adopted by the Puritans after the Reformation in England, when saints' names fell out of favour. Popular until the 19th century, it is presently uncommon.

Amy *f.*

From the French, meaning 'beloved'. There was a 13th-century saint with the Latin form of the name, *Amata*, who made the name fairly popular. In the 19th century, Sir Walter Scott's novel *Kenilworth*, about Amy Robsart, the tragic wife of the Earl of Leicester, made the name fashionable. *Aimée* is the French original of this name.

Amynta *see* Araminta

Anaïs *f.*

A French name which comes from the Greek word for 'fruitful'.

Anastasia *f.*

From the Greek meaning 'resurrection'. The name of a 4th-century saint and martyr, it became fashionable in England in the 13th century, though it was usually abbreviated to Anstey or Anstice, which survive today as surnames. It has always been very popular in Russia, and a daughter of the last Tsar of Russia, called Anastasia, is said to have escaped from the massacre in which the rest of her family died in 1918. Several books, plays and films have been written about her, and they have made the name better known in Britain in the 20th century. **Stacey** and **Tansy** started as a pet forms of this name.

Andrew *m.*, Andrea *f.*

From the Greek for 'manly'. Andrew is the name of the Apostle who is patron saint of Scotland, Russia and Greece, and it first appears in England in the Domesday Book. It has been used in Britain continuously and has enjoyed particular favour in Scotland. The diminutives include *Andy*, *Dandy* (Scots) and **Drew**, which is also used as an independent name. The Italian form, *Andrea*, is actually a boy's name in Italy, but is used as a girl's name in this country. The French boy's form, *André*, is likewise sometimes used for girls, although the more correct form *Andrée* is also used. Other female forms include *Andrene*, *Andrena* and *Andreana*, while *Andra* is both a traditional Scots form of the boy's name and used for girls.

Aneirin *see* Aneurin

Aneka, Aneke, An(n)ika *see* Anne

Aneurin *m.*

This name is traditionally interpreted as the Welsh form of Latin *Honorius*, meaning 'honourable', and is one of the oldest names still in use is Britain. It also appears in the form *Aneirin*. Short forms are *Nye* and *Neirin*.

Angela *f.*

From the Latin *angelus* originally derived from the Greek word meaning 'messenger', hence our word 'angel'. In England it was used regularly as a girl's name, side by side with the masculine form **Angel**, until it was barred as impious by the Puritans. *Angelica* is an old literary form. Angela was revived in the 19th century, together with *Angeline* and *Angelina*. *Angelique* is a French form.

Angharad *f.*

A Welsh name meaning 'much loved'. It is an important name in early Welsh literature, and has been in use since at least the 9th century. The stress is on the second syllable.

Angus *m.*

From the Gaelic *Aonghas*, meaning 'one choice'. It appears in Irish legend in the form

Aengus or *Oengus*, but is more common in Scotland. The name became associated with the classical myth of **Aeneas** (which is close to the Irish pronunciation) in the 15th century, and this form was also used.

Anita, Ann, Anna *see* Anne

Annabel *f.*
Together with *Annabelle* or *Annabella,* this is probably from the Latin *amabilis* meaning 'lovable', a variant of **Amabel**. It is found in Scotland earlier than **Anne**, so it is unlikely to be a form of that name, though it is now sometimes thought of as a compound of Anna and the Latin *bella* meaning 'beautiful'. Diminutives include *Bel, Belle* and *Bella.*

Anne *f.*
From the Hebrew **Hannah**, meaning 'God has favoured me'. The French form Anne or *Ann,* traditionally the name of the mother of the Virgin Mary, was introduced into Britain in the 13th century and the name has enjoyed great popularity since. The spelling with a final 'e' is currently slightly more popular than that without, but the form *Anna* is now much more

popular than either. Pet forms include *Nan,*
Nanette, **Nanny**, **Nancy** and *Annie*, as well as
the variants *Anita, Annette* and *Anona*
(although this, with its pet form *Nona* can be
Welsh in origin). Ann(e) has often formed part
of compounds such as Mary Ann(e). *Anneke* is
the Dutch pet form more often spelt *Anneka* in
this country to reflect the Dutch pronunciation
(*Aneke, Aneka* and *An(n)ika* are also found);
Anya is from the Spanish pronunciation of the
name and *Anouk* a Russian form.

Annes, Annice, Annis *see* Agnes

Annette, Annie *see* Anne

Annora *see* Honoria

Anona, Anouk *see* Anne

Anthea *f.*
From the Greek *antheos*, meaning 'flowery'. This
name seems to have been introduced by the
pastoral poets of the 17th century and it has
been in use ever since, although it was not until
the 20th century that it became very widely
known.

Ant(h)ony *m.*, Antonia *f.*

A Roman family name. Its most famous member was Marcus Antonius, the Mark Antony of Shakespeare's *Julius Caesar* and *Antony and Cleopatra*. The name was very popular in the Middle Ages as a result of the influence of St Antony the Great and St Antony of Padua. The alternative and commoner spelling *Anthony* was introduced after the Renaissance, when it was incorrectly thought that the name was derived from the Greek *anthos* meaning 'flower', as in **Anthea**. The usual short form is *Tony*, which is also used for the female forms *Antonia* and the French *Antoinette*. Feminine short forms, *Toni* and *Tonya* are also found, and *Toinette, Net* and *Nettie* are pet forms of Antoinette. *Anton*, a Continental form of the name, is now also used for boys.

Anya *see* Anne

Aoife *see* Eve

Aonghus *see* Aeneas, Angus

Aphra *f.*

From the Hebrew word meaning 'dust'. It is best

known from the playwright, novelist and spy, Mrs Aphra Behn (1644-89), said to have been the first woman in England to earn her living as a writer. It is also spelt *Afra*.

April *see* Avril

Arabella *f.*
A possible variant of **Amabel**, though it could be derived from the Latin for 'obliging'. It used to be a predominantly Scottish name, particularly in the forms *Arabel* and *Arabelle*. It can be shortened to *Bel, Belle* and *Bella*.

Araminta *f.*
This name appears to have been invented by Sir John Vanbrugh (1644-1726) to use in one of his plays. It may have been influenced by *Aminta* or *Amynta*, an ancient Greek name meaning 'protector'. They all share the short forms *Minta* and *Minty*.

Archibald *m.*
From the Old German words meaning 'truly bold'. The Old English form was used in East Anglia before the Norman Conquest. Thereafter, it was primarily Scottish, and was associated

particularly with the Douglas and Campbell families. The most usual diminutive is *Archie*, now sometimes given to a child rather than the full name. Both forms are enjoying something of a revival at the moment.

Aretha *f.*

Aretha or *Areta* is the Greek word for 'virtue'. It is not a usual name, but has become well known through the singer, Aretha Franklin.

Ariadne *f.*

This is an ancient Greek name meaning 'the very holy one' which probably originally belonged to a goddess. In Greek mythology Ariadne was the daughter of King Minos of Crete and helped Theseus to escape from the labyrinth. The French and Italian forms *Ariane* and *Arianna* are also found.

Arlene *f.*

Arleen or *Arline* is a modern name which probably comes from the final sounds of such names as **Charlene** or **Marlene**.

Armand, Armin, Arminel, Arminelle *see* Herman

Arnold *m.*

From the Old German *Arnwalt*, meaning 'eagle's power'. It appeared in various forms, both Germanic and French, in the Middle Ages, but dropped out of use from the 17th until the late 19th centuries when it had a revival.

Art *see* Arthur

Artemisia *f.*

From the Greek meaning 'belonging to Artemis'. *Artemis* was the Greek goddess of wild animals, vegetation, childbirth and the hunt, comparable to the Roman **Diana**. Artemisia was the name of the queen of Caria in the 4th century BC, who built the Mausoleum at Halicarnassus for her husband. She was also celebrated as a botanist and medical researcher. The name was first used in Britain in the 18th century and still survives.

Arthur *m.*

The origin of this name is disputed. Possible sources are the Celtic word for 'bear' and the Roman name *Artorius*. Whatever its source, its use comes entirely from the fame of its first known bearer, King Arthur. Victorian interest in things medieval made the name popular in the 19th century when one of Queen Victoria's sons was christened Arthur. Over-use in the late 19th and first quarter of the 20th centuries led to a decline, but there are now distinct signs of a revival in popularity. *Art* or *Arty* is used as a short form, particularly in America.

Asa *m.*
From the Hebrew word meaning 'physician'. It is particularly used in the North of England.

Asher *m.*
The name of one of the tribes of Israel. It means 'happy'. Although it is an unusual name, there are signs that its use is on the increase, along with other names from the Bible. It is, of course, also a common surname, and some uses may be from this.

Ashley *m. and f.*
A place and surname, meaning 'ash-field'; it is also used as a first name. It is very popular in Australia and in the United States, where its popularity may be connected with its use as a man's name in *Gone with the Wind*. It is also found as *Ashleigh*.

Ashling *see* Aisling

Astrid *f.*
From the Old German words meaning 'god' and 'beauty'. The name of the wife of St Olaf of Norway, it has long been popular in Scandinavia, and has been used in Britain in the 20th century.

Atalanta *f.*
In ancient Greek myth, Atalanta was a beautiful maiden who wanted to remain single. Since she was a very fast runner, she responded to pressure to marry by saying that she would wed any man who could out-run her, but any losers must die. Many men died in the attempt, but she was finally beaten by one suitor who threw golden apples in her path during the race, and managed to overtake her while she stopped to pick them up.

Athene *f.*
This is the name of the Greek goddess of war, crafts and wisdom. In Britain, it has been used occasionally as a girl's name, as has the Roman form of the name, *Athena*.

Athol *m. and f.*

Athol or **Atholl** is the Scottish place name, used as a first name. The place name means 'New Ireland'.

Aubrey *m.*

From the Old German meaning 'elf ruler'. In medieval romance the diminutive **Auberon** was used and which Shakespeare adopted as **Oberon** in *A Midsummer Night's Dream*. The German form, **Alberic,** developed first into Albery and later into Aubrey.

Audrey *f.*

A shortened form of **Etheldreda**, the Old English for 'noble strength' and one of the sources of **Ethel**. St Etheldreda was a 7th-century Anglo-Saxon princess who founded a religious house at Ely, which later developed into the cathedral that now stands on the site. She was a very popular saint and many churches are still dedicated to her.

Augusta *f.*, Augustus *m.*

From the Latin for 'venerable'. Augustus was a title given to the first Roman Emperor and **Augusta** is its feminine form. *Augustine*, the name of two important saints, one of whom converted the English to Christianity, is another form of the name. It was so popular in the Middle Ages it developed the shorter forms *Austin, Austyn* or *Austen*. *Augustina* is a feminine form of Augustine. *Gus* and *Gussie* are pet forms and this group of names is beginning to become popular once more.

Aurelia *f.*
From the Latin *aurelius* meaning 'golden'. It has been used since the 17th century, and recently a short form, *Auriol*, *Auriel*, *Oriel* or *Oriole* has shown some popularity. The boy's form is *Aurelius*.

Aurora *see* Dawn

Austen, Austin, Austyn *see* Augusta

Ava *f.*
This name is of obscure origin, but probably started life as a pet form of names beginning Av-. It was made famous by the film star Ava Gardner, and is more commonly found in the USA than Britain.

Aveline *see* **Evelyne**

Averil *f. and m.*

Probably from the Old English *eofor* ('boar') and *hild* ('battle'), which appears as *Everild, Everilda* in the 7th century. It was regularly in use until the 17th century, since when it has been less common. Averil is often confused with **Avril** which originally was an entirely different name.

Avis *f.*

The origin of this name, which was popular in England in the Middle Ages, is obscure. It occurred only rarely between the 16th and 19th centuries and was sometimes spelt *Avice*. It is now a rare name.

Avril *f.*

The French for *April*. The name has been popular in the 20th century, mainly for girls born in that month (see also **Averil**).

Axel *m.*

The Scandinavian form of the Old Testament *Absalom*. Its probable meaning, 'father of peace', seems ironic for King David's rebellious son. Axel was introduced to the United States by

Scandinavian immigrants, and it is more common there than in Britain. There is a rare feminine form, *Axelle*.

Ayesha *f.*

From the Arabic meaning 'woman'. It was the name of the prophet Muhammad's favourite wife. In Rider Haggard's novel *She*, it is the name of 'She who must be obeyed'. It is also spelt *Aisha* and *Ayeisha* and even *Iesha*.

Aylmer *see* Elmer

Aylwin *see* Alvin

B

Bab, Babs *see* **Barbara**

Babette *see* **Elizabeth**

Bairre *see* **Barry**

Barbara *f.*
From the Greek *barbaros*, meaning 'strange' or
'foreign', and associated with St Barbara, a 3rd-
century martyr. The name was little used after
the Reformation, but in the 20th century it
became popular again. Abbreviations include
Bab, *Babs* and *Barbie*. The variant form *Barbra*
was publicized by Barbra Streisand.

Barnabas *m.*
is from the Hebrew meaning 'son of exhortation
or consolation', and best known as the name of
the New Testament companion of St Paul. The

diminutive, *Barnaby*, is rather popular at the moment, more so than the full form. *Barney* is a short form shared with **Bernard**.

Barney *see* **Barnabas, Bernard**

Barry *m.*

The English form of a variety of Celtic names, most prominently *Bairre*, a pet form of the Irish *Finbar* (*Finnbar*, *Fionnbharr*) meaning 'fair-haired'. Barry can also be spelt *Barrie*.

Bartholomew *m.*

From the Hebrew, meaning 'son of Talmai', Talmai meaning 'full of furrows'. It was the surname of the Apostle **Nathaniel**. It was very popular in the Middle Ages when the cult of St Bartholomew was at its height. St Bartholomew's Hospital in London was founded in the 12th century and a riotous annual Bartholomew Fair was held in the city to provide funds for it, which was only suppressed in the 19th century. The name is still in use, and has short forms *Bart*, *Barty* and *Bat*.

Basil m.

From the Greek *basileios*, meaning 'kingly'. It

was probably brought to England by the Crusaders, and it has remained in use ever since. Diminutives include *Bas* or *Baz*, and *Basie* and *Bazza* and there are two feminine forms, *Basilia* and *Basilie*. These were common in the Middle Ages, but are hardly ever found today.

Bastian, Bastien *see* Sebastian

Bat *see* Bartholomew

Baz, Bazza *see* Basil

Bea, Beatty *see* Beatrice

Beata *f.*
From the Latin *beatus* meaning 'blessed' or 'happy'. It is both a name in its own right and used as a pet form of **Beatrice**.

Beatrice *f.*
From the Latin *Beatrix*, meaning 'bringer of happiness'. It has strong literary associations. Dante's Beatrice is probably best known, but Shakespeare also used the name in *Much Ado About Nothing*. Recently, both forms of the name have shown signs of returning to popularity, no

doubt helped by the publicity given to it as the name of one of the Duke and Duchess of York's daughters. Short forms include *Bea* or *Bee*, **Beata**, **Beatty** , *Triss* and *Trixie*. There is also a Welsh variant, *Bettrys*.

Becky *see* **Rebecca**

Bee *see* **Beatrice**

Bel *see* **Annabel, Arabella, Belinda, Isabel**

Belinda *f.*
From an Old German name, the latter part of which means 'a snake' (see **Linda**), the first part of which is obscure, but which is commonly thought of as representing the French 'fair'. Its popular use began in the 18th century when it was used in plays by Congreve and Vanbrugh, and in Pope's poem *The Rape of the Lock*. Short forms include *Bel* and all forms of **Linda**.

Bella, Belle *see* **Annabel, Arabella, Isabel**

Ben *see* **Benjamin**

Benedict *m.*
From the Latin *benedictus*, meaning 'blessed',

and most familiar as the name of St Benedict, founder of the Benedictine Order. It was common in medieval England in the forms *Bennet* and *Benedick*. The latter is the name of a character in Shakespeare's *Much Ado About Nothing*. There are feminine forms *Benedicta*, *Benedetta* and a Spanish-American form *Benita*.

Benjamin *m.*

From the Hebrew, meaning 'son of the south' or 'right hand', which might imply strength and good fortune. The Old Testament story of Benjamin, son of Jacob, gave the name the added implications of a favoured, youngest son. The commonest pet forms are *Ben, Bennie, Benny, Benjie* and *Benjy*. It is currently a very popular name.

Bennet *see* Benedict

Bennie, Benny *see* Benjamin

Berenice *f.*

From the Greek *Pherenice* , meaning 'bringer of victory'. It was spread by the imperial conquests of Alexander the Great over Europe and Asia. It was especially popular in Egypt, during the period of Macedonian rule, and its use spread also to the family of Herod of Judea. *Bernice* is a modern form of the name, and *Bunny* is sometimes used as a pet form (see also **Veronica**).

Bernadette *f.*

The commonest female form of **Bernard**. Its use has spread due to the fame of St Bernadette of Lourdes, who lived in the mid-19th century and whose visions started the pilgrimages of healing to that town. The Italian *Bernardetta* has been shortened to *Detta*, which can be used as an independent name. *Bernadine* is another form of the name, and *Bernie* the short form.

Bernard *m.*

A Germanic name meaning 'brave as a bear'. It was very popular in the Middle Ages. Two important saints bearing the name were St Bernard of Menthon after whom St Bernard dogs are named, and St Bernard of Clairvaux who inspired the Second Crusade. It has remained in use ever since. The most usual short forms are *Bernie* and *Barney* which is shared with **Barnabas**.

Bernardetta *see* **Bernadette**

Bernice *see* **Berenice**

Bernie *see* **Bernadette, Bernard**

Berry *see* **Bertram**

Bert, Bertie *m.*
A pet form of a wide number of names including **Albert**, **Bertram**, **Bertrand**, **Gilbert**, **Herbert**, **Hubert**, **Robert**. In all of these cases, the '-bert' part of the name is a Germanic element meaning 'bright'. The name is sometimes used as a given name, when it may take the form *Burt*.

Bertha *f.*
From the Old German word *beraht*, meaning 'bright'. The first famous English Bertha was the wife of King Ethelbert of Kent who welcomed St Augustine to England. In the Middle Ages both Bertha and *Berta* were popular, and the name has been regularly used since, although it is rather uncommon at present.

Bertram *m.*
From the Old German meaning 'bright raven',

the bird associated with the god Odin. The name has been used in England since the early Middle Ages, and has the short forms **Bert** and *Bertie*, and the less common *Berry*.

Bertrand *m.*

This name means 'bright shield' but is often treated as the French form of **Bertram** with which it shares the short forms **Bert** and *Bertie*.

Beryl *f.*

From the gemstone, whose name is related to the Arabic for crystal. It did not appear before the 19th century, and was popular in the early 20th century.

Bess, Bessie, Beth *see* Elizabeth

Betha *see* Bethia

Bethany *f.*

A fairly popular name taken from a New Testament place name, the village where Lazarus lived. The short form *Bethan* is used independently, and is also a short form of **Elizabeth** which has spread from Wales.

Bethia *f.*

Bethia or *Bethea* can be interpreted in three different ways. It can be thought of as a pet form of **Elizabeth**; as a use of the Old Testament place name Bethia, or as an English version of a Gaelic name also found as *Betha*, meaning 'life'.

Betsy, Betty *see* **Elizabeth**

Bettina *f.*

An Italian pet form of **Elizabeth** which was a popular given name in the 1960s.

Bettrys *see* **Beatrice**

Beverl(e)y *m. and f.*

From an Old English surname meaning 'of the beaver-meadow'. It is shortened to *Bev*, and is now only rarely used for boys.

Bevis *m.*

This is a French name, possibly meaning 'bow', introduced into England at the Norman Conquest. It was popular in the Middle Ages and revived again after Richard Jeffries' *Bevis, the Story of a Boy* was published in 1882.

Bianca *see* **Blanche**

Bidelia, Biddy *see* **Bridget**

Bill *see* **William**

Billie, Billy *m. and f.*
This pet form of the boy's name **William** is being used increasingly as a girl's name particularly in America, usually in combination to produce names such as *Billie-Jean* or *Billy Joe*

Birgitta *see* **Bridget**

Blaise *m.*
From the French, meaning either one who comes from the region of Blois, or derived from the Latin for 'stammerer'. It is also spelt *Blase* and *Blaze*.

Blake *m. and f.*
A surname, from the Old English meaning 'black, dark-complexioned', used as a first name.

Blanche *f.*
This is a French name which was brought to England in the 13th century. It means 'white' or

'fair-skinned'. The Spanish and Italian form *Bianca* was used by Shakespeare, and is now rather more popular than the older form.

Blase, Blaze *see* Blaise

Blodwen *f.*
From the Welsh for 'white flower'. It is rarely found outside Wales. *Blodeuwedd*, 'flower form', is the name of a beautiful but unfaithful woman in Welsh medieval romance, while *Blodyn* or *Blodeyn* is the more simple 'flower'.

Blossom *see* Fleur

Bob *see* Robert

Bobbie, Bobby *m. and f.*
These pet forms of **Robert** and **Roberta** are used as names in their own right, and in combinations such as *Bobby Joe*.

Bonnie, Bonny *f.*
This is the Scottish word for 'pretty' used as a first name. Like so many modern names, it probably owes its spread to its appearance in *Gone with the Wind*.

Boris *m.*

From the Russian word for 'fight'. It has been used in Britain and North America in the 20th century, possibly due to cultural influences such as Moussorgsky's opera *Boris Godunov*, the film actor, Boris Karloff, and the author of *Dr Zhivago*, Boris Pasternak, as well as a result of the large number of Slavic immigrants who have come to the two countries.

Bradley *m.*

A surname from the Old English, meaning 'wide meadow', used as a first name. *Brad(d)* is a short form.

Bram *see* Abraham

Brand *see* Brenda

Brandan, Brandon *see* Brendan

Brenda *f.*

Probably a feminine form of the Norse name *Brand*, meaning 'a sword', found in the Shetlands. It was used by Walter Scott in his novel *The Pirate*. However, in practice, it has been used more frequently as a feminine form of **Brendan**.

Brendan *m.*

An Irish name meaning either 'with stinking hair', or, according to one authority, from the Welsh word meaning 'prince'. It is most famously found in the 6th-century Irish St Brendan the Navigator, credited in legend with the discovery of America. It is today particularly popular in Ireland, Australia and the USA. The form *Brandan* or *Brandon* has a long history as an alternative form of Brendan, but can also come from an Old English place and surname meaning 'a hill where broom grows'.

Bret(t) *m.*

From an Old French word meaning 'a Briton' or 'a Breton'. It was given some currency in the last century by the American author Bret Harte.

Brian *m.*

A Celtic name, the origin of which is obscure, though it may be derived from words meaning 'hill' or 'strength'. It was known mainly in Celtic areas until the Norman Conquest, when it was introduced to England. Brian Boru was a famous

Irish King of the 11th century, who defeated the invading Vikings. The name continued to be popular in England until Tudor times, but after that it disappeared until it was reintroduced from Ireland in the 18th century. Today the spellings **Bryan**, **Brien** and **Brion** are also found. There is a rare feminine form **Brianna**, but **Bryony** is more frequently used as an equivalent name for girls.

Bridget *f.*

Brigit was the ancient Irish goddess of poetry whose name meant 'strength'. Her name was borne by 5th-century St Brigit of Kildare, the most revered of the Irish female saints. The Irish name also appears in the forms *Bri(d)gid* and *Bride* (which reflects the Irish pronunciation of the name, with a long 'ee' sound and no 'g'), with the diminutives *Bridie* and *Biddy* and the rather elegant elaboration *Bidelia*. There is also a Swedish saint *Birgitta* or *Brigitta* whose feast day falls on the same day as St Brigit's, and her name has influenced the most common English form of the name, Bridget. *Britt* is a pet form of the Swedish name.

Brien *see* **Brian**

Brigid, Brigit, Brigitta see **Bridget**

Brin see **Bryn**

Brion see **Brian**

Briony see **Bryony**

Britt see **Bridget**

Bronwen *f.*
From the Welsh words meaning 'white breast'.
This name has long been popular in Wales
where it has strong associations with ancient
legend.

Brooke *m. and f.*
The surname meaning 'a brook', used as a first
name.

Bruce *m.*
A French surname which came to Britain at the
time of the Norman Conquest. Members of the
family moved to Scotland and one, Robert
Bruce, became King of Scotland, and was the
ancestor of the Stuart Kings. It has only been
used as a first name since the 19th century. It
has in the past been so popular in Australia that

it has almost become a nickname for an Australian. *Brucie* is a pet form.

Bruno *m.*

This is a German name meaning 'brown', probably imported to this country via the United States where it has been established for longer.

Bryan *see* Brian

Bryn *m.*

A Welsh name, originally describing where someone lived, meaning 'hill'. It can be found as *Brin*, and *Brynmor* ('large hill') is also used.

Bryony *f.*

Bryony or *Briony*, is the name of the climbing hedgerow plant used as a name. The word comes from ancient Greek and means 'to grow luxuriantly'. It is a rather insignificant plant, although it has pretty berries, and the name probably owes its popularity to the fact that it can be used as a female equivalent to **Brian**.

Buck *m.*

Buck was a popular term in the 18th century for a dashing or fashionably-dressed man. It is

usually used as a nickname rather than a true
first name.

Buddy *m.*
This word for a friend is occasionally used as a
first name, but is usually a nickname. The singer
Buddy Holly, for example, was christened
Charles.

Bunny *see* **Berenice**

Bunty *f.*
This was a traditional name for a pet lamb,
which came into use for girls after 1911, when it
was used in a very successful play called *Bunty
Pulls the Strings*. However, it is used more
commonly as a nickname.

Burt *see* **Bert**

C

Caddy *see* **Caroline**

Cadfael *m.*
A Welsh name, meaning 'battle metal', recently given publicity as the name of the hero of the novels of Ellis Peters.

Cadwallader *m.*
From the Welsh for 'battle chief'; it is one of several names with the Welsh word for battle as its root. It is found in Wales and North America.

Cahal *see* **Carol**

Cai *see* **Caius**

Caitlin *see* **Katharine**

Caius, Gaius *m.*
A Roman first name, meaning 'rejoice', which is

still used occasionally. The Welsh name *Cai, Kai* or *Kay*, well known as the name of Sir Kay, King Arthur's foster-brother, is derived from this.

Caleb *m.*

From the Hebrew *kalebh*, meaning 'dog' or 'intrepid'. It first appeared in England in the 16th century and is now more usually found in North America than Britain.

Calliope *f.*

The name of the ancient Greek Muse of epic poetry whose name meant 'beautiful face'. The final 'e' is pronounced. It is not a common name, but is sometimes found in the short form *Cally*.

Calum *m.*

This name was adopted by the Irish from the Latin meaning 'dove'. It was introduced to Scotland in the 6th century with the arrival of St *Columba*. *Callum*, *Colum* and *Colm*, currently particulaly favoured in Ireland, are also found. **Malcolm** comes from this name.

Calvin *m.*

From the surname of the 16th-century French

65

religious reformer Jean Cauvin or Chauvin, latinized to Calvinus, and adopted as a first name by Protestants. It may be derived from the Old French *chauve* meaning 'bald'. It is most commonly found in North America and Scotland.

Cameron *m*.

From the Gaelic meaning 'crooked nose'. It is the name of a famous Scottish clan, although its use as a first name has now spread from Scotland.

Camilla *f*.

A name from Roman legend. Camilla was Queen of the Volsci, a great warrior and exceptionally swift runner. The name may be Etruscan, and possibly means 'one who helps at sacrifices'. It was first recorded in Britain as early as 1205 and at the moment is still popular. *Camille* is the French form of the name, which can be used for either sex, and *Milla*, *Milly* and *Millie* can be used as short forms.

Candice, Candace *f*.

This is an ancient title of the Queen of Ethiopia. It is also spelt *Candis*; *Candy* is a short form.

Candida *f.*

From the Latin meaning 'white'. It was the name of several saints, amongst them one from Naples whom St Paul is said to have cured. The name was not used in Britain until the early 20th century and its introduction was probably due to G.B. Shaw's play, *Candida*.

Candis, Candy *see* Candice

Cara *f.*

An Italian word meaning 'dear' which has been given as a first name in Britain in the 20th century. There is also a variant *Carita*, derived from the Latin meaning 'beloved'. *Carina* is an Italian diminutive (see also **Karen**).

Caradoc *m.*

From the Welsh for 'beloved'. It is common in Wales, but not in other parts of Britain. In the form Caratacus, the name of a Briton who fought against the Romans in the first century, it is one of the earliest recorded British names.

Cari *see* Ceri

Carina, Carita *see* Cara

Carl, Karl *m*. Carla *f*.

These are German forms of **Charles**. The names
have been in general use in America most of
this century, and from there spread to Britain.
The feminines *Carla*, *Carlie* or *Carly* (more
rarely *Karla*) can also be found as forms of the
names found under **Caroline**.

Carlo *see* Caroline

Carlotta *see* Charlotte

Carlton, Charlton *m*.

These names are both forms of an Old English
place name and, later, a surname meaning
'countryman's farm'.

Carly *see* Carl

Carlyn *see* Caroline

Carmel *f*.

From the Hebrew meaning 'garden', and the
name of a mountain famous for its lush
vegetation near the city of Haifa in Israel. St
Louis founded the church and convent on this
mountain which, as legend has it, the Virgin

Mary and infant Jesus often visited. *Carmen* is the Spanish form of the name, *Carmela* the Italian, and *Carmelita* and *Carmelina* pet forms. Carmen is also the Latin word for song, and some people like to think of it in this sense, hence such modern coinages as *Carmina*, the Latin for 'songs'.

Caro *see* Caroline

Carol *f. and m.*
The female forms of the name, which include *Karel*, *Carola* and *Caryl*, were originally pet forms of **Caroline**, but are now popular names in their own right. As a boy's name, this can be an English form of the Irish *Cathal* or in its phonetic spelling, *Cahal* ('battle-mighty') and also an anglicized form of the Latin *Carolus* and Slav *Karel*. Its use has spread to Britain from North America. It is an uncommon male name.

Caroline, Carolyn *f.*
These names come from *Carolina*, the Italian feminine form of *Carlo*, the equivalent of **Charles**. The name was introduced into Britain from Southern Germany by Queen Caroline of Brandenburg-Anspach, wife of George II. Both

forms have been used steadily since the 18th century. Derivatives are *Carla* (see **Carl**),*Carlyn*, **Carol**, *Carola, Carole*. Abbreviations include *Carrie*, **Caddy**, *Caro* and **Lyn**, and Carol.

Carolus *see* **Carol, Charles**

Caron *see* **Karen**

Carrie *see* **Caroline**

Carwen, Carwyn *see* **Ceri**

Cary *m.*
A surname which was only rarely used as a first name until it became famous through the film star Cary Grant. Ultimately, it probably goes back to one of a number of Irish surnames, possibly meaning 'battle-king' or 'dark brown'.

Caryl *see* **Carol**

Caryn *see* **Karen**

Carys *see* **Ceri**

Casey *m. and f.*
This comes from an Irish surname meaning

'vigilant in war'. It is more usual as a boy's
name than as a girl's name. It can also be a
form of the name *Casimir*, 'proclamation of
peace'. This has a female form *Casimira*. Both
can also be spelt with a 'K'.

Caspar *see* Jasper

Cassandra *f.*
In Greek literature this was the name of a
prophetess and princess of Troy. She foretold
the truth, but was never believed. It first became
popular in the Middle Ages and the name has
continued in use ever since. Also found are
Cassandry and abbreviations *Cassie* and *Cass*.
The latter also occurs as a masculine name,
when it may come from an Irish name meaning
'curly-haired'.

Cassia *see* Kezia(h)

Cassie *see* Cassandra

Cathal *see* Carol

Catharine, Catherine, Cathleen, Cathy *see* Katharine

Catriona *f.*

A Gaelic form of **Katharine**. It was the title of a book by Robert Louis Stevenson, and became very popular in the 19th century as a result of this. *Catrina*, *Katrina* and *Katrine* are other forms of the name, and it becomes *Catrin* in Welsh. *Riona* is an Irish pet form.

Cecil, Cecily *see* Cecilia

Cecil *m.*

From the Latin meaning 'blind'. It was the name of a famous Roman clan and was first adopted into English as a girl's name. The popularity of the name in its masculine form only became marked in the 19th century, probably as one of several aristocratic surnames which it was then fashionable to use as first names.

Cecilia *f.*

The female version of **Cecil**. It was the name of a 2nd-century martyr and saint, the patroness of music. The name was first introduced into Britain by the Normans. Variant forms of the name are *Cicely*, *Cecily*, *Sisley*, *Cecil* and the French *Cécile* (used for boys and girls in France). The popular shortened form *Celia* (which can also be derived from another Roman name, Coelia) probably came into fashion as a result of the Celia in Shakespeare's play *As You Like It*. Other abbreviated forms are *Sis*, *Ciss* and *Cissy* or *Sissy* (see also **Sheila**).

Cedric *m.*

This name seems to have been a creation of Sir Walter Scott's for a character in the novel *Ivanhoe*. Scott is said to have used it by mistake for Cerdic who was the first king of the West Saxons. However, as there is a Welsh name *Cedrych* ('pattern of generosity'), it may well be from this. Cedric became popular with parents as a result of the book *Little Lord Fauntleroy* (1886) by F.H. Burnett whose hero bore that name, and it may well also owe its fall in popularity to its association with this book, and the smugly virtuous image of its hero.

Celeste *f.*

From the Latin, meaning 'heavenly'. This name, and its diminutive *Celestine*, are more common in France where the influence of the 13th-century saint, Celestine, may have been greater than in Britain.

Celia see **Cecilia**

Celina, Céline see **Selina**

Cenydd see **Kenneth**

Ceri *f.*

A popular Welsh name, sometimes spelt *Keri* to reflect its pronunciation with a hard 'c'. It comes from the Welsh word for 'love' as do **Cerian, Cerys** or **Carys** and **Cari**. **Carwen** is 'fair love' and has a masculine form, **Carwyn** (see also **Kerry**).

Ceridwen *f.*

This name probably comes from the Welsh words for 'poetry' and 'white, blessed'. It was the name of a Celtic goddess who was said to inspire poetry and was the mother of the great poet, *Taliesin* ('radiant brow'). It is pronounced with a hard 'c' and is generally confined to Wales.

Cerys see **Ceri**

Chad *m.*

The name (of uncertain meaning) of a 7th-century saint who was Bishop of Lichfield. The name has become quite popular in America in the 20th century. A famous holder of the name was the Rev. Chad Varah, founder of The Samaritans.

Chae *see* **Charles**

Chantal *f.*

This is a French name which has only been in use since the beginning of this century. It was the surname of the 16th-century saint, Jeanne-Françoise de Chantal, this surname meaning 'stone'. It has been popular in the United States, where it has developed forms such as *Chantalle* and *Chantelle*. It is pronounced with a 'sh' sound at the beginning.

Charis *f.*

From the Greek meaning 'grace'. The 'ch' is pronounced as a 'k'. It was first used as a first name in the 17th century, although in the 16th century the poet Edmund Spenser in the *Faerie Queen* used the form *Charissa* which has been quite popular in the USA. *Chrissa* can be a short form of this or belong under the **Christine** group of names. There may be some overlap between the

names under **Ceri** and Charis in some users'
minds, since they are pronounced so similarly.

Charity *f.*
From the Latin *caritas*, meaning 'Christian love'.
Translated into English as charity, it was
adopted when it became the custom for
Puritans to name childen after the Christian
virtues. The name Charity was shortened to
Cherry, and is the source of this name. Another
abbreviation is *Chattie*, used also for **Charlotte**.

Charlene *f.*
A feminine form of **Charles** introduced in this
century. It may owe something to *Charline*, a
Dutch form of **Charlotte**. *Charleen* and
Sharlene are also used (see also **Arlene**).

Charles *m.*
Originally from the Old German *carl*, meaning
'man'. It was latinized as *Carolus* and then
changed by the French to Charles. The Normans
brought the name to England, but it did not
become popular until its use by the Stuart kings
of England caused it to be taken up by Royalists
in the 17th century and Jacobites in the 18th
century. Its popularity has continued ever since.

The pet form *Charlie* is now quite common as the given form of the name. *Chas*, originally a written abbreviation, has now come to be used as a short form. *Chuck* is also used, and in Scotland *Chae* or *Chay*.

Charline *see* Charlene

Charlotte *f.*

is the French female form of **Charles**. It was introduced into Britain from France in the early 17th century. Goethe's heroine from the romantic novel, *The Sorrows of Werther*, and Princess Charlotte, daughter of George IV, increased the name's popularity. Abbreviations are *Lottie*, *Lotty*, *Totty*, *Charlie* and *Chattie*, and spellings such as *Sharlott* have been recorded. It has been one of the most popular girl's names for a number of years. *Carlotta* is the Italian form.

Charlton *see* Carlton

Charmaine *f.*

A 20th-century name of rather obscure origin. It may well be a form of **Charmian**, from the Greek, meaning 'joy'. This was the name of one of Cleopatra's attendants in Shakespeare's *Antony and Cleopatra*. Strictly speaking, Charmian should be pronounced with a hard 'c', but the 'sh' pronunciation is also found. Charmaine is sometimes spelt *Sharmaine*.

Chas *see* Charles

Chattie *see* Charity, Charlotte

Chay *see* Charles

Chelsie *f.*
This name, which is beginning to be used in Britain having been popular for some time in the United States, seems to be from the place name *Chelsea*, a form that is also used. The re-spelling is presumably because it then fits in with other girl's names ending '-ie' such as *Elsie* (see **Elsa**). Chelsea means 'landing-place for limestone', but its use is probably because of the glamorous and fashionable image that this part of London enjoys.

Cherie *f.*
The French word for 'darling'. The forms *Sherry*, *Sheree* and *Sherrie* are phonetic spellings. *Cher*

can be the French for 'dear' or a short form of
Cheryl; *Cherida* is a development of the name,
possibly influenced by the Spanish for 'dear',
querida.

Cheralyn, Cherilyn *see* Cheryl

Cherry *see* Charity

Cheryl *f.*

This is probably a development of the name
Cherry (see **Charity**). Other forms of the name
are *Cheralyn*, *Cherilyn*, *Sheril* and *Sheryl*, and
Cher can be a short form (see also **Cherie**).
These names only came into general use in the
1940s, but rapidly became popular.

Chester *m.*

A surname taken from the English town, used as
a first name. The word comes from the Latin for
'fort'.

Chevonne *see* Sheena

Chip *see* Christopher

Chloe *f.*

From the Greek, meaning 'a green shoot', a

name given to the goddess Demeter who protected the green fields. It was a popular name in classical literature which was picked up by the Elizabethan poets. It is becoming steadily more popular at the moment. *Chloris*, 'greenish', is another name from Greek myth, and was again associated with fertility. It is sometimes spelt *Cloris*, to reflect the pronunciation of these names with a hard 'c'.

Chris *see* Christabel, Christine, Christopher

Chrissa *see* Charis, Christine

Chrissie, Chrissy *see* Christabel, Christine

Christabel *f.*
This name was first used in Britain in the 16th century, and is thought to be a combination of 'Christ' and the Latin *bella* to mean 'beautiful Christian'. It is not a common name in Britain, although it is sometimes used in memory of the suffragette, Dame Christabel Pankhurst. It is also spelt *Christobel* and abbreviated forms are *Chris*, *Chrissy*, *Chrissie* or *Christie*.

Christel, Christen see Christine

Christian *m. and f.*

This name, with its transparent meaning, has been used in Britain since the 13th century. It became more popular after its use by Bunyan for the hero of *Pilgrim's Progress*, but has never been as common as the feminine form, **Christine**, although it is currently enjoying some popularity as a boy's name.

Christiana see Christine

Christie see Christabel, Christopher

Christine *f*

The commonest of the many girl's names meaning 'a Christian'. *Christen* is probably the oldest form, followed by *Christiana*. Others are *Christina*, *Christian(n)e*, a feminine form of **Christian**, the Welsh form *Crystin*, and spellings such as *Krystyna*, *Kristina*, *Krista*, *Kristin*. The German form, *Christel,* may have helped the development of the name **Crystal**. Short forms are *Chrissie*, *Chrissy* and *Chris* and further variants will be found under the Scottish pet form, **Kirsty**. *Chrissa*, *Chryssa* or *Kryssa* can be thought of either as a part of this group or as a short form of Charissa (see **Charis**).

Christmas *see* Noel

Christopher *m*
From the Greek meaning 'bearing Christ'. As a first name it is used in honour of the saint who was believed to have carried the infant Christ to safety across a river. Thus St Christopher was the patron saint of travellers. The popularity of the name in Britain has fluctuated since the 13th century when it was first used, but it is a popular choice at the moment. The Scottish equivalent of the name was *Chrystal* or **Crystal**. Abbreviated forms are *Kester*, *Kit*, *Chip* and *Chris*. *Christie* or *Christy* is a pet form particularly used in Ireland.

Chryssa *see* Christine

Chrystal *see* Christopher, Crystal

Chuck *see* Charles

Ciara, Ciaran *see* Kieran

Cicely *see* Cecilia

Ciera, Cieran *see* **Kieran**

Cilla *see* **Priscilla**

Cimmie *see* **Cynthia**

Cindy *f*
A short form of names such as **Lucinda** and
Cynthia, now used as an independent name. It
is also spelt *Cindi* and *Cindie*.

Ciss, Cissy *see* **Cecilia**

Clare, Claire *f*
From the Latin meaning 'clear, famous'. The
religious order of the Sisters of St *Clara* or 'Poor
Clares', founded in the 13th century, was
probably responsible for the rapid spread of the
name throughout Europe. The name has been
popular for some time, with the spelling Clare
currently more popular than the French form,
Claire. Among the many derivatives are *Claribel*
and *Clarinda,* which can be shortened to
Clarrie.

Clarence *m.*
In the 14th century King Edward III's son,

Lionel, married the heiress of the town of Clare in Suffolk. He was later created Duke of Clarence, the name Clarence meaning 'of Clare'. This title seems to have been first used as a name in the early 19th century in Maria Edgeworth's novel *Helen*.

Claribel *see* Clare

Clarice *see* Clarissa

Clarinda *see* Clare

Clarissa *f.*
From the Latin meaning 'brightest, most famous'. It was made popular in the 18th century by Samuel Richardson's novel *Clarissa Harlowe*. **Clarice** is an older form of the name. They share the abbreviation **Clarrie** with Clara.

Clark *m.*
The surname meaning 'a clerk,' used as a first name. Famous users were the actor Clark Gable, and in fiction, Clark Kent, the everyday name for Superman.

Clarrie *see* Clare, Clarissa

Claud *m.*

From the Roman name, *Claudius*, itself derived
from the Latin meaning 'lame'. In homage to the
Emperor Claudius, under whom Britain was
conquered by the Romans, the name was used
in this country in the 1st and 2nd centuries. Its
use soon lapsed in Britain though not in France
where it is spelt *Claude* and used for either sex,
and it was from the French that it was taken and
revived in Britain in the 16th century by the
Scottish family of Hamilton. A derivative is
Claudian, and the pet form *Claudie* can be
found.

Claudia *f.*

The female form of **Claud** and at the moment
rather more popular. Two French diminutives
are also used: *Claudette* and *Claudine*, a name
made famous by the novels of Colette.

Claudian, Claudie *see* Claud

Claudius *see* Claud

Claus *see* Nicholas

Clem, Clemmie *see* Clement, Clementina

Clemence, Clemency *f.*

From the Latin meaning 'mildness'. The name first appeared in Britain in the 13th century. All of the group of names with this meaning are enjoying something of a revival, Clemency in particular.

Clement *m.*

From the Latin, meaning 'mild, merciful'. It was the name of an early saint and of several popes. It was popular in Britain from the 12th century until the time of the Reformation, had a revival in the reign of Queen Victoria, and is once again showing signs of popularity. Its abbreviated forms are *Clem* and *Clemmie*.

Clementina, Clementine *f.*

These names are the feminines of **Clement**, with which it shares short forms. Clementine was originally a German form, fashionable during the 19th century, and is now showing signs of returning to popularity.

Cleo *f.*

A shortened form of *Cleopatra,* from the Greek meaning 'glory of her father'. The famous

Egyptian queen of this name died in 30 BC and it did not take long for her name to become a byword for sexual allure and tragic love.

Clidna *see* Cliona

Clifford *m.*
There are several places named Clifford ('ford by the cliff') in Britain, any of which could become a surname. Towards the end of the 19th century the surname came into use as a first name. It is now most often used in its short form *Cliff*.

Clint *m.*
A short form of *Clinton*, an aristocratic surname meaning 'farm by the river Glyme', used as a first name. The short form has been given fame by the actor, Clint Eastwood.

Cliona *f.*
The the name of a beautiful fairy-woman in Irish legend. Her name can also be spelt *Clidna,* *Cliodhna* or *Cliodna* .

Clive *m.*
A surname meaning 'dweller by the cliff' which has come to be used as a first name, probably in

honour of Robert Clive, known as Clive of India, who was prominent in the British conquest of India.

Clodagh *f.*

The name of a river in Ireland. It was first used in the 20th century as a first name by the Marquis of Waterford for his daughter. Its use has now spread beyond Ireland.

Cloris *see* Chloe

Clotilda *f.*

An Old German name meaning 'loud battle'. Clotilda was a queen of France in the 6th century who converted her husband, King Clovis (see **Lewis**) to Christianity. The name is not common.

Clover *f.*

This is the flower name used as a first name. Its spread may have been helped by its use for one of the Carr sisters in Susan Coolidge's *Katy* books. Names such as *Clova* can be interpreted either as a re-spelling of Clover, or as a feminine form of *Clovis* (see **Lewis**).

Clovis *see* **Lewis**

Clyde *m.*

This Scottish river name meaning 'the washer'
is a very ancient one, in use since before the
Roman occupation. It may well have been the
name of the local goddess. It came to be used as
a surname, then as a first name.

Cody *m.*

This is said to be an Irish surname meaning
'descendant of a helpful person'. It has been
popular in the United States, where it is also a
place name and well-known as the surname of
the Wild West hero, Buffalo Bill Cody. *Codey* and
spellings with 'K' have also been recorded. It is
occasionally used for girls.

Coinneach *see* **Kenneth**

Colette *f.*

From a French diminutive of **Nicola**. It was the
name of the 15th-century reformer of the 'Poor
Clares' religious order. The name is best known
in this country as the pen-name of a 20th-
century French writer. It is also spelt *Collette*.

Colin m.

This has a similar origin as **Colette**, for it was a French pet form of **Nicholas**. In Scotland, it was also interpreted as coming from the Gaelic word *cailean*, meaning 'puppy' or 'youth'. After a considerable period of popularity, the name is not much used for boys at the moment. There are rare feminine forms *Colina* and *Colinette*.

Colleen f.

The Irish word for 'girl' used as a first name. The name is not widely used in Britain, but is fairly common in North America.

Collette *see* Colette

Colm, Colum, Columba *see* Calum

Con, Conchobar, Conchobhar *see* Conor

Conan m.

From the Irish, meaning 'hound, wolf'. It is not very common outside Ireland today. The most famous holder of the name was Sir Arthur Conan Doyle, creator of Sherlock Holmes, but the name is probably best known today from the fictional stories and films of *Conan the*

Barbarian. Although the fictional character's name is pronounced in the American films with the same sound as in 'cone', in Ireland the name is pronounced with a short 'o'.

Conor *m.*

From the ancient Irish name *Conchobar* or *Conchobhar* meaning 'lover of hounds'. It was the name of one of the great kings in Irish heroic stories, and has long been a popular name in Ireland. It can be spelt *Connor*, and shortened to *Con* or *Conny* and sometimes *Conn*, which is also a separate name, perhaps meaning 'wisdom'. It shares its short forms with **Conan**.

Connie *see* Constance

Connor, Conny *see* Conor

Conrad *m.*

From the Old German words for 'bold counsel'. The name is found mostly in Germany where in the 13th century Duke Conrad was a greatly beloved figure. Objection to his public execution by the conquering Charles of Anjou led to a widespread use of this name in German-speaking states. Examples of it have been found in Britain since the 15th century. *Curt* or *Kurt* is a short form used as an independent name, now used rather more frequently than the full form.

Constance *f.*

Constance and its Latin form, *Constantia*, mean 'constancy'. The name became popular in many parts of Christendom after Constantine the Great ordered the toleration of Christianity in the Roman Empire, AD 313. It was introduced into England at the time of the Norman Conquest. The form Constancy was used by the Puritans in the 17th century while Constantia became popular in the 18th century. *Constantina* is another form of the name. Constance has been out of fashion since the early part of the century, but there has recently been a sudden surge of interest in its use. Its abbreviation is *Connie*.

Constantine *m.*

From the Latin, meaning 'firm, constant'. It was the name of the first Christian Emperor, and so became popular with Christians. Three Scottish kings were named Constantine after a Cornish saint who was believed to have converted their ancestors to Christianity in the 6th century. It became popular in England from the 12th to the 17th centuries, and was the origin of the surnames Constantine, Considine, Costain and Costin. It is not widely used in Britain today. The composer *Constant* Lambert (1905-51) shows an English form of the name.

Cora *f.*

From *kore*, the Greek word for 'girl, maiden'. The name did not appear in Britain until the 19th century, although it was in use in North America earlier on. The diminutive, **Corinna**, has a much longer record of use.

Coral *f.*

This name reflects the beauty and value of the substance, and was popular earlier this century. A French form which is also in use in Britain is **Coralie**.

Cordelia *f.*

This name first appeared as *Cordeilla* in the 16th-century chronicles of Holinshed, from which Shakespeare altered the name to Cordelia for his play *King Lear*. The name is probably a form of *Cordula*, the name of one of the virgins martyred with St Ursula. It probably comes from the Latin word for 'heart'.

Corey *m.*

This is a surname of unknown meaning which has come to be used as a first name. It has been popular in the United States for a number of years, and is just beginning to show up here. It is also spelt *Cory*, and in forms such as *Corrie* has been used for girls, especially in combination with other names. Spellings beginning with 'K' are also found.

Corinna *f.*

This name comes from the Greek word *kore* meaning 'girl, maiden', a name given to the goddess **Persephone** who was associated with the coming of spring. Ovid's use of the name in his love poetry probably inspired its use among 17th-century poets, particularly Herrick. The French form, *Corinne* is also used. *Corin,* much used in poetry as the name for a love-sick shepherd, is the male form of the name, occasionally also used for girls (see also **Cora**).

Corisande *f.*

This is a name full of glamour and romance,

having been the name of a fair maiden in a medieval romance and a poetic name given to Diane de Poitiers, the powerful and influential mistress of the 16th-century king, Henry II of France, who was famous for her beauty.

Cormac *m.*

This Irish name is of doubtful meaning, although it is sometimes said to mean 'a charioteer'. It appears frequently in Irish legend, but through its prevalence in early Irish history and the Irish Church, the name was accepted as having a Christian character in Ireland and remained in steady use. A variant is *Cormick*.

Cornelius *m.*, Cornelia *f.*

From the Latin *cornu* meaning 'a horn', and were the male and female forms of the name of a famous Roman clan. The male version has never been particularly common in England, but was used in Ireland as a substitute for the native *Conchobar* (see **Conor**). Its abbreviated forms are *Corney*, *Corny* and *Cornie*. Cornelia is slightly more used, but still uncommon.

Corrie, Cory *see* Corey

Cosmo m.

From the Greek *kosmos*, meaning 'order'. It is the name of one of the two patron saints of Milan and was used by the famous Italian family of Medici in the form *Cosimo* from the 14th century onwards. It was the name of the 3rd Duke of Gordon who was a friend of Cosimo III, Grand Duke of Tuscany, and the name was introduced into several other Scottish families. It is not common in Britain today, but can be found, together with its feminine form *Cosima*.

Courtney m. and f.

An aristocratic surname used as a first name. It comes from *Courtnay*, a French place name, although the name is often interpreted as from 'court nez' the French for 'short nose'.

Craig m.

The place and surname meaning 'crag', used as a first name.

Cressida f.

Cressida is comes from a misreading of the name Briseida, 'daughter of Brisis', who appears in Homer's account of the Trojan War. In the 14th century, the Italian Boccaccio used the name, and it was adapted by Chaucer in his verse-novel *Troilus and Criseyde*; the story of Troilus's undying love for the fair Cressida, set against the background of the Trojan War. Shakespeare changed the name to Cressida for his version of the story. Despite the fictional character's faithlessness in love, the name has recently become quite popular. An abbreviated form is *Cressy*.

Crispin, Crispian *m*.

From the Latin *crispus*, meaning 'curled'. The 3rd-century martyrs Crispinus and Crispinianus were the patron saints of shoemakers. Crispin was popular in Britain in the Middle Ages and has recently enjoyed a revival.

Crystal *f*.

While this looks like, and is no doubt mainly used as, another jewel name, the spread of this name may have been helped by **Christel** the German form of **Christine**. Crystal is also spelt *Chrystal* and the form *Krystal* has become known through the television series *Dynasty*. As a man's name it is a pet form of **Christopher**.

Crystin *see* **Christine**

Cudbert, Cuddy *see* Cuthbert

Curt *see* Conrad

Curtis *m.*

A surname, from the French meaning 'courteous', used as a first name. It has been used more frequently in the United States than in Britain.

Cuthbert *m.*

From the Old English words *cuth* and *beorht*, meaning 'famous' and 'bright'. It was in common use both before and after the Norman Conquest, and was the name of a 7th-century saint and Bishop of Lindisfarne, Northumbria. It sometimes appeared as **Cudbert**, and had the pet form **Cuddy**. The name fell out of use just after the Reformation until the 19th century, when it was brought back by the Oxford Movement. It was a slang term for someone who avoided military service during the First World War, and it may be partly due to this usage that the name is not popular today. The school 'swot' in the *Beano*'s Bash Street Kids is called Cuthbert Cringeworthy.

Cy *see* **Cyril, Cyrus**

Cybill *see* **Sybil**

Cynthia *f.*
One of the titles of the Greek goddess Artemis
(see **Artemisia**), meaning 'of Mount Cynthus',
reputedly one of her favourite places. It first
became known as a name through its use by the
Latin poet Propertius, and it was later popular
among Elizabethan poets. Mrs Gaskell's character in her novel *Wives and Daughters* brought it
back into favour during the late 19th century.
Pet forms include **Cindy**, *Cindi* or *Cindie* and the
rare *Cimmie*.

Cyprian *m.*
From the Latin *Cyprianus* meaning 'from
Cyprus'. It was the name of a Christian martyr of
the 3rd century.

Cyra *see* **Cyrus**

Cyril *m.*
From the Greek *kyrios*, meaning 'lord'. There
were two saints of this name in the 4th and 5th
centuries, and it was a 9th-century Saint Cyril

who took Christianity to the Slavs, and devised
the Russian Cyrillic alphabet. The name was
first used in England in the 17th century, but did
not become common until the 19th century. The
name shares the abbreviation *Cy* with **Cyrus**,
and has been recorded spelt *Syril*. There is a
rare feminine form *Cyrilla*.

Cyrus *m.*

A Greek form of the Persian word meaning 'sun'
or 'throne'. This is the name of the founder of
the Persian Empire in the 6th century BC, as
well as a number of other Persian kings. It was
first used in Britain in the 17th century among
Puritans, probably in honour of the fact that the
Emperor Cyrus allowed the Jews to return to
Palestine from their Babylonian captivity. It is
quite popular in North America, where the short
forms are *Cy* and *Cyro,* and is beginning to be
more used over here. There is a feminine form
Cyra.

D

Daffodil *f.*
One of the less common flower names, but is still to be found from time to time.

Dafydd, Dai *see* **David**

Daisy *f.*
Possibly a 19th-century pet name for **Margaret**, a pun on *marguerite*, the French word for daisy. However, there is no reason why it should not have come into use as a simple flower name, and few people today would use it otherwise.

Daithi *see* **David**

Dale *m. and f.*
The Old English for 'valley'. At first more common as a girl's name, it is now more frequently used for boys.

Damaris *f.*

The Greek name in the New Testament of an Athenian woman converted by St Paul. This led to it being adopted by the Puritans in the 17th century. It is probably a form of a Greek name meaning 'heifer'.

Damhnait *see* Dymphna

Damian, Damien *m.*

From the Greek, meaning 'tamer'. There have been four saints called by this name. It was little used in this country before this century, but became popular in the 1970s.

Damon *m.*

From the Greek, meaning 'to rule' or 'guide'. In Greek legend, Damon and Pythias were inseparable friends, famous for their willingness to die for each other.

Dan *see* Daniel

Dana *m. and f.*

As a boy's name this comes from the surname, the Old English word for a Dane, and is some-times found in the form *Dane*. The actor Dana

Andrews made it well known, but it is now unusual as a man's name. The female name is either a Scandinavian girl's form of **Daniel**, or, in Ireland, taken from the pagan fertility goddess, Dana or Ana.

Dandy *see* **Andrew**

Daniel *m.*, Danielle *f.*

Daniel is the Hebrew name of an Old Testament prophet, meaning 'God has judged'. It was found in England before the Norman Conquest, but only among priests and monks. It became more widespread in the 13th and 14th centuries. In Ireland and Wales it is often found as a transliteration of the Irish *Domhnall* (see **Donald**) and Welsh *Deiniol*, meaning 'attractive, charming'. Its shortened forms are *Dan* and *Danny*. For girls, *Danielle* is the most common form, but *Daniel(l)a* and even *Danette* are used.

Daphne *f.*

From the Greek for 'bay tree, laurel'. In classical mythology, it was the name of a nymph whom the god Apollo loved. In seeking to escape his attentions she called on the gods for help, and was changed by them into a laurel. The name was a traditional name for dogs until the turn of the century, when it became quite common as a girl's name.

Daria *f.*

This is the more common female form of *Darius*. Darius was the name of the 6th-century BC king of the Persians who was defeated by the Athenians at Marathon. The name means 'protector'.

Darlene *f.*

This appears to be a modern invention, made up of the first syllable of one of the names beginning Dar-, or perhaps from 'darling', with the -ene ending that is popular with newly created names such as **Charlene** and *Raelene*.

Darrel(l) *m. and f.*

Also spelt *Dar(r)yl*, this is another surname used as a first name. In this case the surname comes from a French village, the village name meaning 'courtyard, open space'. Originally mainly a boy's name, its spread as a girl's name may owe something to Enid Blyton's use of her second husband's surname, Darrell, for the heroine of her *Malory Towers* school stories.

Darren *m.*

A surname of unknown meaning used as a first name. It seems to have been introduced in the 1950s and become popular in the 1960s. *Darran* is also used.

Darryl, Daryl *see* **Darrell**

David *m.*

The Hebrew name of the second king of Israel in the Old Testament, meaning 'beloved'. This name absorbed the Celtic *Daithi*, meaning 'nimbleness' (the 'th' is pronounced 'h'), and became very popular in Wales and Scotland. The patron saint of Wales is a 6th-century David. There were Scottish kings of this name in the 10th and 14th centuries. The name did not appear in England before the Norman Conquest, but it was a common medieval surname in the variant forms Davy, Davit and Deakin. Short forms are *Dave*, *Davy*, *Davie* and in Wales, *Dafydd* becomes *Dai* or *Taffy*, the latter being an English nickname for a Welshman.

Davida, Davina *f.*

These Scottish female forms of **David** are found from the 17th century, but were not much used

until about thirty years ago, when they started
to become more popular. They are sometimes
shortened to *Vida* and *Vina* and *Davita* and
Davinia are also found.

Davie, Davy *see* David

Dawn *f.*
This name came into use in the late 19th
century. *Aurora*, the name of the Greek goddess
of dawn, had been in vogue slightly earlier and
the English translation was probably a literary
invention. In the 20th century, it was popular
among starlets, and therefore gained publicity
and a large following for some years.

Dean *m.*
A surname, meaning 'valley', adopted as a first
name. It seems to have become popular in the
United States first, but has been widely used
here since the 1960s.

Deanna, Deanne *see* Diana

Dearbhail *see* Dervla

Deborah *f.*

A Hebrew name meaning 'bee', and the name of a prophetess and poet in the Old Testament. It was first used by the Puritans in the 17th century. *Debbie* or *Debby* is a common abbreviation which is sometimes used independently. *Debra* is a modern spelling of the name.

Decimus *m.*, Decima *f.*

From the Latin meaning 'tenth'. They were used in Victorian times for the tenth child in large families, and are still sometimes used in smaller families. Decimus Burton (1800-81) was a noted architect.

Declan *m.*

The name of an early Irish saint associated with Ardmore. It has recently been popular with Irish parents.

Dee *m. and f.*

This is usually a nickname, given to anyone with a name beginning with the letter D, but is occasionally found as a given name. Compounds such as *Deedee* also occur.

Deirbhile *see* Dervla

Deiniol *see* Daniel

Deirdre *f.*

The Irish name of a character in Irish and Scottish legend, possibly meaning 'raging' or 'sorrowful'. 'Deirdre of the Sorrows' left Ireland for Scotland in order to marry the man of her choice, and lived with him and his two brothers near Loch Etive. Tempted back to Ireland by a false offer of friendship, the three men were killed, and Deirdre, in her grief, committed suicide. The name became popular after the late 19th-century Celtic revival, and is currently enjoying another major revival in Ireland.

Del, Dell *see* Delbert, Derek

Delbert *m.*

This name has been in use since at least the beginning of the century. It is probably formed on the pattern of surnames such as *Delroy* ('of the king') and *Delmar*, ('of the sea') which are also used as first names, keeping the Del- part and adding -bert from the many Germanic names which end in it. Short forms *Del* or *Dell* are also used as a first name, and can be a pet form of **Derek**.

Delia *f.*

This name is derived from Delos, the legendary birthplace of the Greek moon goddess Artemis (see **Artemisia**) and a name sometimes given to her. It was popular with pastoral poets in the 17th and 18th centuries.

Della *f.*

Originally a short form of **Adela**, this is now well established as a name in its own right.

Delmar, Delroy *see* Delbert

Demelza *f.*

A place name, meaning 'the hill-fort of Maeldaf', used as a first name in Cornwall. It became more widely known through its use in the *Poldark* books and television series.

Demetrius *m.*

This ancient name means 'follower of Demeter', the Greek goddess of corn and agriculture. It was the name of a highly successful general who died in 286 BC. In the form *Demetrios*, it is the name of a Greek saint and as *Demitrus* it is found in the Bible. *Dimitri* or *Dmitri* is the Russian form of the name. *Demetra*, which can

be shortened to *Demi*, is the commonest form
of the names for girls. The name was little used
by English speakers until fairly recently when it
became fashionable in the USA.

Den *see* Denis

Denholm *m.*

A place name, meaning 'island valley', used as a
first name. The actor, Denholm Elliot, was a
well-known example. The similar *Denham*,
'home in a valley', is also used.

Denis *m.* Denise *f.*

A development of *Dionysos* who was the Greek
god of wine and revelry. Denis or *Dennis*, is the
French form and the name of the patron saint of
France. It occurs in England from the 12th
century on. In Ireland it has long been used as a
substitute for the Irish *Donnchadh* (see
Duncan). *Den* and *Denny* are short forms.
Denise, the female form, is also from French.
Dion (*m.*) and *Dionne* (*f.*) can either come from
Dionysos or be a separate name from the same
root, connected with the word for 'a god', while
Dione can be thought of either as a variant of
Dionne, or as the name of another character

from Greek mythology whose name means 'divine queen'. These are growing in popularity (see also **Dwight**).

Denzil *m.*

In the form *Denzell*, this is an old Cornish surname derived from a place-name. In the 17th century it came by marriage into the Holles family who adopted it as a first name. It is still thought of as mainly a Cornish name.

Derek, Derrick *m.*

From the Old German **Theodoric**, meaning 'people's ruler'. It occurs in the 15th century but has only become popular in the last century. Its fall from favour between these two periods is attributed to a notorious 17th-century hangman of that name. Variants recently revived are *Deryk, Deric* and the Dutch form *Dirk*, popularized by the actor Dirk Bogarde. Pet forms are *Derry, Rick, Rickie* and *Del or Dell*.

Dermot *m.*

This is the anglicized spelling of *Diarm(a)it* or *Diarm(a)id*, the Irish name possibly meaning 'free from envy', or 'free man'. The legendary character who bore this name eloped with

Grainne who was betrothed to **Finn**. Finn pursued the lovers for a long time and finally brought about Dermot's death.

Derrick, Derry *see* Derek

Dervla *f.*
This is the phonetic form of *Deirbhile*, an old Irish name meaning 'daughter of the poet'. It is best known from the travel writer, Dervla Murphy. It also occurs as *Dervila*, reflecting the Irish pronunciation. The similar-looking *Dearbhail*, which can be anglicised *Derval* or *Dervilia* meaning 'daughter of Fal' (a figure in Irish legend) is very popular at the moment.

Deryk *see* Derek

Des, Desi *see* Desmond

Désirée *f.*
A French name meaning 'desired'. It has been in use since the beginning of the Christian era in the Latin form *Desideria*, originally for a long-awaited, much-desired child. The French boy's name, *Didier*, 'longing' shortened to *Didi*, would be the male equivalent

Desmond *m.*

From the Irish *Deas-Mumhain*, meaning '(man) of Desmond' i.e. Munster. It was originally used as a surname in Ireland. Later it became a first name, and came to England in the late 19th century. *Des* and *Desi, Desy, Dezi* are short forms.

Detta *see* Bernadette

Dezi *see* Desmond

Di *see* Diana

Diarm(a)id, Diarm(a)it *see* Dermot

Diana *f.*

The Latin name of the Roman goddess, equivalent to the Greek, Artemis (see **Artemisia**). She was associated with the moon and virginity. She was also the goddess of hunting and protector of wild animals. Its use as a first name dates from the Renaissance, when the French form *Diane* is also first found. *Di* is the commonest short form, as seen in the popular nickname for the Princess of Wales. The actress, *Deanna* Durbin, introduced a different form of the name, and the form *Deanne* is also found, while Diane has developed forms such as *Dianne* and *Dyan(ne)*. **Dinah** is a separate name.

Dick, Dickie, Dickon *see* Richard

Didi, Didier *see* Desirée

Dieudonné, Dieudonnée *see* Donata

Digby *m.*
A place and surname, meaning 'the settlement by the dike', used as a first name.

Dilys *f.*
From the Welsh, meaning 'perfect, genuine'. The name became current in Wales in the 19th century, and is now no longer confined to Wales. *Dilly* is a short form.

Dimitri *see* Demetrius

Dinah *f.*
From the Hebrew, meaning 'lawsuit' or 'judged'. It was the name of one of Jacob's daughters in the Old Testament. It came into use in the 17th century and was a favourite name in the 19th century, when it was often confused with

Diana. Nowadays it is often spelt *Dina*.

Dinsdale *m.*
A place and surname used as a first name. It means 'settlement surrounded by a moat'.

Dion, Dione, Dionne, Dionysos *see* **Denis**

Dirk *see* **Derek**

Djamila *see* **Jamila**

Dmitri *see* **Demetrius**

Dodie, Dodo, Doll, Dolly *see* **Dorothy**

Doireann *see* **Doreen**

Dolores *f.*
This name was originally a short form of the Spanish *Maria de los Dolores*, or 'Mary of the Sorrows', after the feast of the 'Seven Sorrows of Our Lady'. Spain uses other names from titles of the Virgin; *Mercedes* (Our Lady of the Mercies) and *Montserrat*, from Our Lady of Montserrat, a famous monastery. Dolores became popular in North America about 1930. Pet forms are **Lola**, *Lolita* and *Lo*.

Dolph, Dolphus *see* **Adolph**

Domhnall *see* **Daniel, Donald**

Dominic *m.*, **Dominique** *f.*

From the Latin *dominicus* meaning 'of the Lord'. It is possible that the name was first used for children born on a Sunday. It was used in England as a monk's name before the Norman Conquest and probably became more widespread on account of St Dominic, founder of the Order of Preachers known as the Black Friars early in the 13th century. Until this century it was almost exclusively a Roman Catholic name, but is now widely used. *Dominick* is also found, and the name can be shortened to *Dom*. *Dominique*, from the French, is now the most popular form for girls, although *Dominica*, the original Latin feminine form is sometimes used.

Donald *m.*

From the Irish *Domhnall* or *Donal(l)* (the second reflecting the pronunciation, with a long 'o' as in 'doe') meaning 'world mighty', the name of a number of medieval Irish kings. This became Donald in Gaelic. Common short forms are *Don* and *Donny*. Various forms of the name were coined in the Highlands to turn Donald into a girl's name, of which *Donalda* and *Donella* have been the commonest.

Donata *f.*

This name is far more often used than the boy's equivalent, *Donatus* or *Donat*, both names meaning 'given [by God]'. The Old French equivalent of this Latin name was *Dieudonné(e)*, which is still very occasionally found.

Donella *see* Donald

Donna *f.*

This is the Italian word for 'lady'. It has been popular as a first name in the 20th century, particularly in North America. *Madonna*, 'My Lady', in use in the USA by the 1930s, comes from the same word.

Donnchadh *see* Denis, Duncan

Donovan *m.*

An Irish surname, meaning 'dark brown', used as a first name. It gained publicity as the name of a popular singer from the 1960s.

Donny *see* **Donald**

Dora *f.*
Originally this name was a short form of
Dorothy and **Theodora**, but it is now a name in
its own right. It came into use at the beginning
of the 19th century. A pet form is *Dorrie*, shared
with other names like **Doreen** and **Doris**.

Dorcas *f.*
From the Greek for 'gazelle'. In the New
Testament it was used as a Greek translation of
the Aramaic **Tabitha**, the name of the woman
raised from the dead by St Peter. The name was
later used to describe groups of women who
made clothes for the needy.

Doreen *f.*
From the Irish *Doireann*, a name sometimes
found in English spelling as *Dorren*. Its origin is
rather obscure, but in Irish mythology it is the
name of at least two supernatural beings. A
short form is *Dorrie,* and the name can also be
found spelt *Dorinne*.

Dorian *m. and f.*
The ancient Greek people known as the Dorians

came from the northern Greek area called
Doris, but later dominated the south of the
country. The best-known group were the
Spartans. The word was introduced as a first
name by Oscar Wilde in his *The Picture of Dorian
Gray* (1891). Like so many boy's names, it has
recently begun to be used as a girl's name as
well. It is now also spelt *Dorien*, *Dorrien* and for
girls *Dorianne* and *Doriana*.

Dorinda *f.*

This name was invented in the 18th century as a
poetic variation of **Dora** and **Dorothy**. Many
other forms, like **Belinda** and *Clarinda* (see
Clare) were invented at this time.

Dorinne *see* **Doreen**

Doris *f.*

This is the name of a sea nymph in Greek
mythology, possibly meaning 'bountiful', and
also a term for a woman member of the **Dorian**
people of Greece. In classical literature it was
used a poetic name for a lovely woman. It came
into common use at the end of the 19th century
and was popular into the 1930s. A short form is
Dorrie.

Dorothy, Dorothea *f.*

From the Greek meaning 'gift of God'. The name is found in Britain from the end of the 15th century and has been in use ever since. In the 16th century, it was abbreviated to *Doll(y)*, and was so popular that the toy became known as a doll, Doll being such a likely name for a baby. In Scottish dialect, a doll is sometimes called a *Dorrity*. Later short forms are **Dora**, *Dot*, *Dottie*, *Dodo*, *Dodie* and *Thea* (see also **Theodora**).

Dorren *see* **Doreen**

Dorrie *see* **Dora, Doreen, Doris**

Dorrien *see* **Dorian**

Dorrity, Dot, Dottie *see* **Dorothy**

Doug, Dougie *see* **Douglas**

Dougal, Dugal(d) *m.*

From the Irish *dubh ghall*, meaning 'dark stranger', a name given to the Danish Vikings. It was a common first name in the Scottish Highlands, and while it still has strong Scottish associations, it now has a more general use.

Douglas *m.*

From the Gaelic *dubh glas*, meaning 'black stream'. It was first a Celtic river name, then the surname of a powerful Scottish family famous for its strength and bravery in fighting, and then from about the late 16th century a first name for both girls and boys. It is now restricted to boys. *Duggie* and *Doug(ie)* are pet forms.

Drew *m.*

From the Old German *Drogo*, meaning 'to carry' or 'to bear', a name which was brought to Britain by the Normans and later became a surname. This surname, which like any other, can also be used as a first name, can also come from two other sources: as a short form of **Andrew**, probably the commonest source of Drew as a first name, and from an old French word for 'lover'. Parents wishing to use this name may take their choice. It has recently been used occasionally for girls.

Drusilla *f.*

A feminine form of the Latin *Drusus*, a Roman family name, possibly meaning 'firm'. It occurs in the New Testament and was adopted in the

17th century by the Puritans. It is still used occasionally, mainly in North America.

Duane, Dwayne *m.*

An Irish surname, probably meaning 'black', used as a first name. The pop singer, Duane Eddy, made the name better known in the 1950s.

Dudley *m.*

Originally, a surname derived from the place of that name in Worcestershire. The Dudley family rose to power under the Tudors. Robert Dudley, Earl of Leicester, was the favourite of Queen Elizabeth for many years. Like other aristocratic names it was adopted for general use as a first name in the 19th century. *Dud* is used as a short form.

Dugal(d) *see* Dougal

Duggie *see* Douglas

Duke *see* Marmaduke

Dulcie *f.*

Dulcie is a name coined in the 19th century

from the Latin *dulcis*, meaning 'sweet'. There was an earlier name, Dulcibella ('fair and sweet'), which in popular speech became Dowsabel. Dulcie was very popular in the early years of this century, but now has an old-fashioned ring to it.

Duncan *m.*

The Scots form of the Irish ***Donnchadh*** (pronounced **don**-ne-ha, the 'h' ideally the sound in Scottish 'loch'), meaning 'brown '. It was the name of two Scottish kings and at one time was almost entirely confined to Scotland, although this is no longer the case.

Dunstan *m.*

From the Old English words *dun*, meaning 'hill' and *stan*, meaning 'stone'. It was the name of a famous 10th-century Archbishop of Canterbury. It appears from time to time before the Reformation, and was revived by the Oxford Movement in the 19th century.

Dustin *m.*

Best known from the actor Dustin Hoffman, this name has recently been very popular in the United States. It may be from a place name

123

meaning 'dusty', or could be a form of
Thurstan, a Norse name meaning 'Thor's
stone', i.e. an altar dedicated to the thunder god
Thor.

Dwayne *see* Duane

Dwight *m.*
Originally, an English surname, which may go
back to the same source as **Denis**. The use of
this name as a first name in the United States
probably arose from respect for Timothy
Dwight, President of Yale University (1795-
1817). The US President, Dwight D. Eisenhower,
gave a wider circulation to the name.

Dyan, Dyanne *see* Diana

Dylan *m.*
This is the name of a legendary Welsh hero, son
of the sea god, possibly meaning 'son of the
wave'. It was rare outside Wales, but the Welsh
poet, Dylan Thomas, made the name more
familiar to the general public. The singer, Bob
Dylan, often referred to by his second name,
took his stage name from the poet and has
increased its use.

Dymp(h)na *f.*

The anglicized form of the Irish *Damhnait*, the name of an Irish virgin martyr. It means 'fawn, little deer'. The English form is pronounced with a 'pf' or just 'p' in the middle, the Irish name something like 'dav-nit'.

E

Eachan *see* **Hector**

Eadan *see* **Etain**

Eamon(n) *see* **Edmund**

Earl *m.*
From the noble title, in Old English meaning a 'nobleman' or 'chief'. This has been used as a first name in the last hundred years, mainly in North America. *Erle* is a variant spelling, as in the author, Erle Stanley Gardiner.

Earnest *see* **Ernest**

Eartha *f.*
This name comes from the Old English *eorthe*, meaning 'earth'. A well-known modern example is the singer and actress, Eartha Kitt,

but the name is rare outside the southern United States, where **Ertha** and **Erthel** are also found.

Ebenezer *m.*
From the Hebrew, meaning 'stone of help'. In the Old Testament it is the name of a stone which Samuel called Ebenezer, in memory of the triumph of the Jews over the Philistine army and in thanks for God's help. It was first used as a first name in the 17th century among the Puritans. It is now used mainly in North America, with the shortened form **Eben**.

Ed, Eddie *see* Edgar, Edmund, Edward

Edan, Edana *see* Aidan, Edna

Eden *m. and f.*
From the name of the garden created for Adam and Eve in the Bible. In Hebrew it means 'delight'. Like other Old Testament place names, it has been used as a first name since the 17th century when the Puritans first adopted it, but has never been common.

Edgar *m.*
From the Old English meaning 'fortunate spear'.

Owing to the popularity of King Edgar, King Alfred's grandson, the name continued in use after the Norman Conquest, but it faded out at the end of the 13th century. It was then used by Shakespeare for a character in *King Lear*, and revived with other Old English names by 18th-century writers of fiction. Its popularity in the 19th century probably stems from its use for the hero of Scott's novel *The Bride of Lammermoor*. It is now a fairly unusual name, sometimes shortened to *Ed* or *Eddie*.

Edie *see* Edith

Edina *see* Edna

Edith *f.*
From the Old English name Eadgyth, meaning 'fortunate war'. There were at least two English saints of that name in the 10th century. The name survived the Norman Conquest and was probably adopted by the Normans and used to replace several English names. Edith was in use throughout the Middle Ages, after which it became rather rare, but it returned to favour in the 19th and early 20th centuries. Often shortened to *Edie*, it has a rare form, *Editha*.

Edmund *m.*

From the Old English Eadmund, meaning 'happy protection'. It was the name of two kings of England and of two saints. *Edmond* is the French form which was used from the late Middle Ages. *Eamon(n)* is the Irish form. It was well used in the 19th century, then went rather out of fashion, but is now steadily coming back into use. Shortened forms are *Ed, Eddie, Ted* and *Teddy*.

Edna *f.*

One source of this name may be *Edana*, a feminine form of the Irish name *Edan*, meaning 'fire' (see **Aidan**). It has also been connected with a shortened form of Edwina (see **Edwin**), via *Edina*. In addition the name occurs twice in the Apocrypha and its Hebrew meaning is probably 'rejuvenation'. The modern use of it may stem from the popularity of the novelist Edna Lyall in the late 19th century.

Edward *m.*

From the Old English meaning 'fortunate guardian'. Edward the Confessor established its popularity in England and ensured its survival after the Norman Conquest. It was further strengthened by the accession of Edward I, after which there was an Edward on the English throne for over a hundred years. It has remained in use in Britain ever since, and is currently one of the most popular boy's names. The short forms, **Ned** and **Ted**, together with **Neddy** or **Teddy**, have been used since the 14th century, but **Ed** or **Eddie** is more common abbreviated forms found today.

Edwin *m*. Edwina *f*.

From the Old English meaning 'fortunate friend'. This was the name of the first Christian king of Northumbria in the 7th century. The name survived the Norman Conquest and became popular in the 18th century. There has recently been an increase in the number of parents choosing it for their child, particularly as a second name. Edwina is a 19th-century female form, recently given much publicity by the politician, Edwina Currie.

Effie *see* Euphemia

Egbert *m*.

From the Old English meaning 'bright sword'.

This was the name of the first king of a united England and of a 7th-century Northumbrian saint. It enjoyed some degree of popularity in the 19th century, but is now rarely found.

Eibhlin *see* Evelyn

Eileen *f.*

An Irish development of **Evelyn**. Like other Irish names it spread throughout Britain at the beginning of the 20th century. *Eily* is a short form. It is not uncommon to find it spelt *Aileen*.

Eithne *f.*

A name prominent in Irish legend and history, being used by a goddess, a number of queens and no less than nine saints. It means 'kernel' which in old Irish poetry is a term of praise. Modern variants include *Ethne*, *Ethna*, *Eithne*, *Aithne* and the phonetic *Enya*.

Elaine *f.*

An Old French form of **Helen**, which occurs in medieval literature. It came into general use through the popularity of Tennyson's *Idylls of the King* (1859), which is based on Malory's *Morte d'Arthur* and which includes the story of *Lancelot*

131

and Elaine. There is also a Welsh name *Elain*, meaning 'fawn'.

Eleanor *f.*

Elaenor and *Elinor* are French forms of **Helen**, which have been used in this country since the Middle Ages. Eleanor is currently by far the more popular of the two spellings, although Elinor is still regularly used. *Eleanora*, the Italian form which gives us **Leonora**, is also found. Eleanor is shortened to *Ellie*, **Ella**, **Ellen**, **Nell** and **Nora**.

Elena *see* **Helen**

Elfrida *see* **Alfred**

Eli *m.*

From the Hebrew meaning 'elevated'. This name was the name of the high priest in the Old Testament who looked after the prophet Samuel when he was given to the Temple as a baby. It was adopted as a first name in the 17th century. It is also a shortened form of **Elias**, *Eliza* (see **Elizabeth**) and *Elihu*, which means 'God is the Lord').

Elias, Elijah *m.*
From the Hebrew meaning 'Jehovah is God'.
Both forms were very common in the Middle
Ages, with the diminutives *Ellis* and *Eliot* or
Elliot which became surnames now used as first
names.

Elihu *see* **Eli**

Elinor *see* **Eleanor**

Eliot *see* **Elias**

Elizabeth, Elisabeth *f.*
From the Hebrew *Elisheba*, meaning 'oath of
God' or 'God has sworn'. The present form
developed from the Greek *Elisabet* through the
Latin *Elisabetha* to Elizabeth. In Britain the 'z'
form is usual, on the Continent the 's' is used,
although in the Authorized Version of the New
Testament, the name is spelt Elisabeth. It was
first used by members of the Eastern Church,
then found its way across Europe to France,
where it developed the form **Isabel**. This was
also the usual medieval form in England.
Elizabeth became common about the end of the
15th century, and its later popularity in England

stemmed from the long reign of Elizabeth I. Among the many diminutives the following have been most used are: *Bess(ie)*, *Betsy*, *Betty*, *Beth*, (with **Bethan** in Wales, see **Bethan**) *Eliza*, *Lizzy*, *Liz*, *Liza*, *Libby* and the Scottish *Elspeth*, *Elspie* and **Elsie**, which are now used independently. The German **Elsa**, *Lisa*, *Liese* or *Liesel*, the Italian **Bettina**, and the French *Elise*, *Lisette* and *Babette*, are also used in Britain.

Elke *f.*
A German pet form of the name **Alice**. It is found in a slightly different form used by the singer *Elkie* Brooks.

Ella *f.*
A name used by the Normans probably derived from the Old German *Alia*, meaning 'all'. It can also be a pet form of Isabella (see **Isabel**), **Ellen** or **Eleanor** (see also **Luella**).

Ellen *f.*
This is an older English form of **Helen**, now used independently, and also a short form of **Eleanor**. In the past it has been especially popular in Scotland and Ireland and is now showing signs of a wider popularity.

Ellie *see* **Eleanor**

Elliot, Ellis *see* **Elias**

Elmer *m.*

This is a surname which comes from both the
Old English Ethelmer 'noble and famous' and
Ethelward 'noble guard'. It became a first name
in the USA in honour of two brothers with the
surname Elmer who were prominent in the
American War of Independence. *Aylmer* is
another form of the name. While *Elma* is
actually a short form of *Wilhelmina*, a German
feminine of **William**, it can also be used as a
female form of Elmer.

Eloise *f.*

Currently, the more popular version of the name
known to history as *Heloise*. Abelard and
Heloise were two famous and tragic 12th-
century lovers, and Heloise was renowned for
her beauty, intellect and faithfulness in love.
The name can be spelt *Heloïse*, *Eloïse* and
sometimes occurs as *Eloisa*. Experts do not
agree where the name comes from. Some say it
is an Old German name perhaps meaning 'hel-
met power', others say it comes from the same

source as **Lewis** by way of an old southern French name *Aloys, Aloyse* (see **Aloysius**).

Elsa, Elsie *f.*

One source of Elsa is the Old German meaning 'noble one'. However, both names are also used as abbreviations of **Elizabeth**, and Elsie is sometimes a short form of **Alison**. Elsie was originally Scottish and is the more common form in Britain. Elsa is the heroine in Wagner's opera, *Lohengrin*, and this made the name popular in the 19th century.

Elspeth, Elspie *see* Elizabeth

Elton *m.*

A surname, probably meaning 'Ella's settlement', used as a first name. The singer, Elton John, more or less began its use as a first name.

Eluned *f.*

This is a Welsh name connected with the word for 'idol'. It is seldom used outside Wales. The short form *Luned* is the origin of **Lynette.**

Elvira *f.*

A Spanish name, probably introduced by the

conquering Visigoths in the Dark Ages. Its meaning is not clear. It has been used occasionally since the beginning of the 19th century. It is perhaps best known as the name of the ghost in Noel Coward's play, *Blithe Spirit*.

Elvis *m.*

A name that was almost unknown until given world fame by Elvis Presley. It is probably a version of the name of the Irish saint *Ailbhe* (a name which in Irish can be used for either sex, and which is pronounced 'alva') or *Alby*, which is found in Wales in the form St Elvis. Although Presley was not the first member of his family to bear the name, modern uses are all thanks to him.

Emanuel *m.*

From the Hebrew meaning 'God with us'. It was the name given to the promised Messiah by the prophet Isaiah in the Old Testament. It was introduced as a first name by the Greeks in the form *Manuel*. This is also the Spanish form. *Manny* is used as a pet form, and there is a feminine, *Emanuelle*.

Emblem, Emblin *see* Emmeline

Emer *f.*

Emer (pronounced with a long 'ee' at the beginning) is currently one of the more popular Celtic names in Ireland. In legend it was the name of the woman loved by Cuchulainn, the great hero of the Ulster cycle of legends. She is described as having the following six desirable gifts: those of beauty, voice, sweet speech, skill with the needle, wisdom and chastity. It is occasionally found as *Emir*.

Emerald *see* Esmeralda

Emily *f.*

From the Latin Aemilius, the name of a Roman family. Boccaccio, the 14th-century Italian writer, used *Emilia*, popularizing this form in the Middle Ages, and Chaucer borrowed it in the form Emelye. The name has persisted since then, becoming very common as Emily in the 19th century, when it was sometimes shortened to **Emma**. Nowadays, these two names are among the most popular girl's names. *Milly* is a pet form. It may be the popularity of Emily that has led to signs of an increased use of the masculine form *Emil* or *Emile* for boys.

Emir *see* **Emer**

Emlyn *m.*

A common Welsh name, possibly derived from the Latin Aemilius, also the source of **Emily**, but which is more likely to be from a Welsh place-name.

Emma *f.*

A shortened form of Old German compound names beginning *ermen* meaning 'universal' as in the name *Ermyntrude*, 'universal strength'. It was introduced to England by Emma, daughter of Richard I, Duke of Normandy. The English form was Em(m), and this was used until the mid-18th century, when the original form was revived. Jane Austen's novel *Emma* (1816) has also been influential. Today, Emma is one of the commonest girl's names. *Emmy* is a pet form, and Emma is also used as a short form of **Emily**.

Emmeline *f.*

From the Old French pet forms of *Emilia* and **Emily**. The Normans introduced the name to England in the 11th century in many variant forms, like *Emblem* and *Emblin*, but Emmeline is the one most often found.

Emmy see **Emma**

Emrys see **Ambrose**

Ena *f.*
This name can come from a number of sources.
It can be a short form of any name ending with
the sounds -ina or -ena, it can be an English
form of **Eithne**, but its popularity in the last
century came from the affection felt for Queen
Victoria's daughter, Princess Ena, who later
became Queen of Spain. Her name came from
neither of these sources, but was due to a misreading of her intended name 'Eva' at her
christening.

Enid *f.*
This is a Welsh name, meaning 'life, soul', that
came into use in England in the 19th century
through Tennyson's Arthurian poem, *Geraint
and Enid* in the *Idylls of the King* (1859).

Enoch *m.*
From the Hebrew, meaning 'trained, skilled' or
'dedicated'. It was the name of an Old
Testament patriarch and was adopted in the
17th century by the Puritans. It is now rare,

although a well-known modern example is the politician, Enoch Powell.

Enya *see* Eithne

Eoan, Eoghan *see* Eugene

Eoin *see* John

Ephraim *m.*
From the Hebrew meaning 'fruitful', an Old Testament name that was revived in the 17th century by the Puritans. It is seldom used in England, but is still found in North America. *Eph* is a short form.

Eppie *see* Euphemia

Erasmus *m.*
From the Greek, meaning 'beloved, desired', and the name of an early Christian martyr. The Dutch scholar and religious reformer Desiderius Erasmus (1465-1536) made the name famous, although it was used in Britain before his influence was felt. *Erastus* comes from the same root. The short form *Rastus* is better known in Britain and in North America, but the name is rare.

Eric *m.*, Erica *f.*

From Scandinavia; the second syllable means 'ruler', the first is doubtful but possibly means 'ever'. The name was brought to Britain about the 9th century by the Danes. Possibly Dean Farrar's book *Eric or Little by Little* was responsible for its popularity with parents in the 19th century. *Erica*, the feminine form, is now sometimes identified with the Latin botanical name for heather. Both forms are sometimes spelt with a 'k' instead of 'c'. Short forms are *Rick*, *Rickie* or *Ricky*.

Erin *f.*

From the Gaelic *Eireann*, a poetical term for Ireland. It is a modern name, particularly popular in the USA and Australia.

Erle *see* Earl

Ermyntrude *see* Emma

Ernest *m.*

From the Old German, meaning 'vigour' or 'earnestness'. It is sometimes spelt *Earnest*. It was introduced by the Hanoverians in the late 18th century and was common in the 19th century. Oscar Wilde's play, *The Importance of Being Earnest* (1899) increased its popularity. *Ernestine*, the female form, like Ernest, is not very common today. Shortened forms are *Ern* and *Ernie*. The latter is the nickname commonly used in Britain for **E**lectronic **R**andom **N**umber **I**ndicating **E**quipment, the premium bond prize selector.

Errol *m.*

Probably a surname used as a first name, although it is not certain whether the surname is a development of Eral, a medieval form of **Harold**, or whether it is a variant of **Earl**.

Ertha, Erthel *see* **Eartha**

Esmé *m. and f.*

Probably from the French for 'esteemed', but is now usually treated as synonymous with the French *Aimée*, meaning 'beloved' (see **Amy**). It passed from France to Scotland in the 16th century, and then much later to England. It is now more often used as a girl's name, in which case it can also take the forms *Esmée* and *Esma*.

Esmeralda *f.*

The Spanish for 'emerald'. It was used by the French 19th-century writer Victor Hugo for the heroine in his novel *The Hunchback of Notre Dame*, and has occasionally been used since in Britain and France. The English form *Emerald* is also found, as is the form *Esmeraldah*.

Esmond *m.*

From the Old English *east* and *mund*, meaning 'grace' and 'protection'. This name was never common and fell out of use in the 14th century. Its modern use probably dates from Thackeray's novel *The History of Henry Esmond* (1852). It is nowadays rather rare.

Ess, Essie, Essy *see* Esther

Essylt *see* Isolda

Estella *f.*

A blend of the Latin *stella* and the French *étoile*, meaning 'star'. It was a French name given by Charles Dickens to the heroine of *Great Expectations*, and has been used since. *Estelle* is another form of the name. It sometimes shares the shortened forms of **Esther** (see also **Stella**).

Esther *f.*

In the Old Testament, this name is the Persian equivalent of a Hebrew word meaning 'myrtle'. It was frequently used in the form *Hester* and appears in England in the 17th century, adopted by the Puritans. It can also be spelt *Ester*. Shortened forms include *Essy, Essie* and *Ess,* with Hester becoming *Hetty*.

Etain *f.*

In Irish legend *The Wooing of Etain* is the story of the love of the fairy Princess Etain of the Fair Hair for a mortal man. This tale was retold in an opera called *The Immortal Hour* first performed in 1914. The opera was a great success at the time, and led to a use of the name outside Ireland. In Ireland the name is usually *Etan* or *Eadan* and pronounced 'ad-an'.

Ethan *m.*

This is a Hebrew name meaning 'firmness', which occurs several times in the Old Testament. It is more often used in the United States than in Britain.

Ethel *f.*

This name was not originally independent, but

developed in the 19th century as a shortening of various Anglo-Saxon names beginning with the root Ethel-, from *aethel* meaning 'noble' (see **Audrey**).

Ethelbert *see* **Albert**

Etheldreda *see* **Audrey**

Ethna, Ethne *see* **Eithne**

Etta, Ettie *see* **Henrietta**

Euan *see* **Eugene**

Eufemia *see* **Euphemia**

Eugene *m.*, **Eugenie** *f.*

From the Greek meaning 'well-born'. In North America the masculine form is usually abbreviated to **Gene**. The Celtic names *Eoghan* (pronounced 'eoh-un') or *Eoan* ('ohn'), and their Scots form *Ewan* or *Ewen* and *Euan* have traditionally been interpreted as forms of Eugene, although sometimes confused with Eoin, a form of **John**. However, some would claim that they are a native Celtic name meaning 'born of the yew'. *Eugenie*, the French feminine form, came into use from the French Empress Eugénie (1826-1920) who spent the last 50 years of her life in England. *Eugenia* is also used for girls.

Eunice *f.*

From the Greek, meaning 'happy victory'. The name is mentioned in the New Testament and was adopted by the Puritans in the 17th century. In Greek it is pronounced as three syllables, with a hard 'c' and the final 'e' sounded, but modern users soften the 'c' if they use the three-syllable pronunciation or more often use the pronunciation indicated by the phonetic spelling *Unice*.

Euphemia *f.*

From the Greek, meaning 'fair speech' or, by implication, 'silence'. It occurs as *Eufemia* and *Euphemie* from the 12th century. Later it became confined to Scotland, where it is still found, usually abbreviated to *Effie* (very popular at the beginning of the century), *Eppie* or, occasionally, **Fay** or **Phoebe**.

Eustace *m.*

From the Greek meaning 'rich in corn' and hence 'fruitful' generally. Because of the two

147

saints Eustachius, this name was in use in Britain before the Norman Conquest and was popular from the 12th to the 16th centuries. *Eustacia*, the female form, was used in the 18th and 19th centuries but is now rare. A short form, **Stacey** (or *Stacy*), is now a name in its own right.

Eva *see* Eve

Evadne *f.*
This is a Greek name of uncertain meaning. It was used occasionally in the early part of the 20th century and has become better known recently because of the character of Evadne Hinge of the Hinge and Brackett comic duo.

Evaline *see* Evelyn

Evan *m.*
This is a Welsh form of **John**, the anglicized form of the Welsh spelt variously *Iefan*, *Ifan* or *Ieuan*. In Scotland it is also an anglicized form of the Irish Eoghan (see **Eugene**).

Evangeline *f.*
From the Greek meaning 'bringer of good

news', the same word that gives us 'evangelist'. It was first introduced by Longfellow for his poem *Evangeline* (1847), and still tends to have a rather literary flavour. *Evangelina* is also found.

Eve *f.*

From the Hebrew meaning 'life', and in the Old Testament this is the name of the first woman. *Eva* is the Latin form, Eve the English. It was in use in Britain even before the Reformation, when Old Testament names were not generally popular. In Ireland it was used as a substitute for the earlier Gaelic *Aoife* (pronounced 'ee-fa'), meaning 'radiant', currently a very popular name. The pet form of Eve is *Evie* and *Evita* is a Spanish pet form (see also **Zoë**).

Evelyn *f. and m.*

When the Normans conquered Ireland they brought with them a girl's name *Aveline*, meaning 'wished for (child)'. This was adopted by the Irish in the form *Eibhlin* (pronounced either with the 'bh' as a 'v', or silent, giving **Eileen**), which in turn was anglicized *Eveline* or *Eveleen* and later developed forms such as *Evaline*, *Evelena* and *Evelina*. It was also adopted as a surname, usually spelt Evelyn, and some time

149

around the 17th century this surname started to be used for boy's. As a boy's name Evelyn is the usual spelling; all forms are used for girls.

Everard *m*.

From the Old German for 'brave boar'. The name was brought to Britain by the Normans and was fairly common in England in the 12th and 13th centuries and has been used occasionally ever since. In Scotland, it became *Ewart*. The surname *Everett* comes from Everard, and has sometimes been used as a first name

Everild, Everilda *see* Averil

Evie, Evita *see* Eve

Ewan, Ewen *see* Eugene

Ewart *see* Everard

Ezekiel *m*.

From the Hebrew meaning 'may God strengthen'. It is the name of an Old Testament prophet, and was used from the 17th century in Britain. It is still current in North America and is beginning to re-appear here. *Zeke* is the usual short form.

Ezra *m.*

From the Hebrew, meaning 'help' and the name
of the author of one of the books of the Old
Testament. It was adopted as a first name by the
Puritans in the 17th century. The name is no
longer common, but a well-known example
from the 20th century is the American poet,
Ezra Pound.

F

Fabian *m.*

From the Latin family name *Fabianus*, possibly meaning 'bean-grower'. There was a pope of this name and a St Fabian in the 3rd century, and there is a record of the name being used by a sub-prior of St Albans in the 13th century. There is little other evidence of it until the 16th century, but its use as a surname shows that it was known previously. The Roman general *Fabius*, known as the 'delayer' for his tactics of waiting for the right moment to achieve his ends rather than rushing in, was the inspiration for the Fabian Society, a socialist society founded in 1884. A female form, *Fabienne*, comes from the French *Fabien*. There is a Spanish female form *Fabiola*.

Faith *f.*

One of the Christian virtues used as names after the Reformation. It was formerly used for both sexes, but is now a girl's name. **Fay** is a short form.

Fanny *see* **Frances, Myfanwy**

Fatima *f.*
This is an Arabic name which means either 'chaste' or 'motherly'. It was the name of the Prophet Muhammad's favourite daughter, the only one of his children to have children of her own. It has been popular in the USA with Black Muslims. It is also occasionally used in a Christian context in honour of Our Lady of Fatima.

Faustine *f.*
Fausta and *Faustus* were names given to his twin children by the ancient Roman dictator, Sulla. The names mean 'fortunate' and Sulla had always considered himself particularly blessed with good luck, taking the nickname **Felix**. Faustine is the French form of the name. Although the two girls' names are sometimes used, the legend of Dr Faustus who sells his soul to the Devil, has made it difficult to use the boy's name.

Fawn *f.*
The word for a young deer used as a first name.

Fay *f.*

A short form of both **Faith** and **Euphemia**, and also an old form of the word 'faith'. In addition it is an old version of the French word for 'fairy' found in the name of the Arthurian enchantress Morgana le Fay. It was in use by 1872, at least in fiction. It is also spelt *Faye*.

Feargus *see* **Fergus**

Fedelm, Feidhelm *see* **Fidelma**

Felice, Felicia *see* **Felix**

Felicity *f.*

From the Latin *felicitas*, meaning 'happiness'. It was the name of two saints and was used by the Puritans in the 17th century.

Felix *m.*, Felicia *f.*

From the Latin meaning 'happy, lucky'. Felix was widely used in the Middle Ages and had a fairly strong hold in Ireland, where it was used to replace the Irish *Phelim*. It is currently enjoying a revival in popularity. The female form, Felicia, has a long history of use and was also very popular in the Middle Ages. *Felice* was a variant form.

Fenella *f.*

A Gaelic name meaning 'white-shouldered'. The name became known in Britain in the 19th century as a result of Sir Walter Scott's novel *Peveril of the Peak*. The Irish form of the name is **Finola** or **Fionnuala** (pronounced 'Fin-noola'), which can be shortened to **Nola** or **Nuala**. Some years ago the Scottish form was the more popular choice, but this has probably now been overtaken by the Irish.

Ferdinand *m.*

From the Old German words meaning 'brave journey'. The name was never popular in Germany but was common in Spain, especially in the forms Fernando and Hernando. Short forms are **Ferd, Ferdie** and occasionally **Nandy**. At the moment the name is being used slightly more often than before.

Fergal *m.*

This is an Irish name meaning 'valorous'. The surnames Farrell and Farall, which come from it, reflect the Irish pronunciation.

Fergus *m.*

Fergus or **Feargus** come from the Irish words for

'man' and 'strength'. It is a fairly common first name in Scotland and Ireland and is also used in the North of England. *Fergie* is a short form.

Fern *f.*
The plant name used as a first name.

Fi *see* Fiona

Fidelma *f.*
This is the more usual form of the Irish name *Fedelm* or *Feidhelm* (pronounced 'fed-elm' in modern Irish). Its meaning is not clear, but several of the early women who bore the name were famous for their beauty.

Fifi *see* Josephine

Finbar, Finnbar, Fionnbharr *see* Barry

Fingal *m.*
This is the name given to the Scottish legendary hero (the equivalent of the Irish **Finn**), who figures in the 18h-century Ossianic poetry. He was a mighty warrior, a defender of the underdog and righter of wrongs. Fingal's Cave is named after him. The name means 'blond stranger' and was a term used of the Vikings (see also **Morven**).

Finn

Finn or *Fionn* is an Irish name meaning 'white, fair'. Finn Mac Coul (Finn mac Cumaill) is a great hero of Irish mythology and folklore. He was chosen to lead the Fenians (an elite armed troop) because of his truthfulness, wisdom and generosity, but he was also of great physical strength. However, all this did not prevent Finn's fiancée Grainne from running away with his companion, **Dermot**. *Finnian* or *Finian* comes from the same root, and was the name of a 6th-century British saint and *Fintan* means either 'white ancient one' or 'white fire'. These two names can also be used as pet forms of Finbar (see **Barry**).

Finola *see* Fenella

Fintan *see* Finn

Fiona *f.*

From Gaelic, meaning 'fair, white'. It was first used in the 19th century by William Sharp as a pen name (Fiona Macleod). He modelled it on the Irish man's name *Fionn* or *Finn*. It was long thought of as a particularly Scotish name, but is now used throughout the English-speaking world. *Fi* is the short form.

Fionn *see* **Finn**

Fionnuala *see* **Fenella**

Flann *m.*
This is an Irish name meaning 'red' that would have started life as a nickname. *Flannan* started as a pet form of this.

Flavia *f.*
A Roman family name, which probably meant something like 'golden or tawny-haired'. See also **Fulvia**

Fleur *f.*
The French word for 'flower'. It was first used as a name in the 20th century, in John Galsworthy's series of novels, *The Forsyte Saga*. The English equivalents *Flower* and *Blossom* are also found.

Flip *see* **Philip**

Flo, Floy *see* **Florence**

Flora *f.*
From the Latin meaning 'flower'. Flora was the Roman goddess of flowers and the spring. The name was once particularly associated with the

Scottish Highlands because of Flora Macdonald who played an important part in the escape of Bonnie Prince Charlie after the Battle of Culloden in 1746. The male equivalent names *Florent* and *Florian* are now little used in Britain but are found on the Continent.

Florence *f.*

comes from the Latin name *Florentius*, derived from the word meaning 'blooming'. In the Middle Ages, Florence was used as often for men as for women, but it has since ceased to be used as a man's name. Florence Nightingale was named after the town in Italy where she was born, and her fame popularized the name in the 19th century. Abbreviated forms are *Florrie*, *Flossie*, *Floy* and *Flo*.

Florent, Florian *see* Flora

Florrie, Flossie *see* Florence

Flower *see* Fleur

Floyd *see* Lloyd

Frances *f.*

This name derives from from *Francesca,* the femi-

nine form of the Italian *Francesco* (see **Francis**). It was first used in Italy in the 13th century, about the same time as the French form *Françoise* began to appear. *Francine* is another French form. Frances was not used in Britain until the 15th century, and it became popular with the English aristocracy at the time of the Tudors. The short forms are *Fanny*, *Fran*, *Francie* and *Frankie*. Francesca is, at the moment, the most popular choice from this group among parents.

Francis *m.*

From the Latin meaning 'little Frenchman'. The name became popular in Europe in the 13th century because of St Francis of Assisi. The Italian word *Francesco* was the saint's nickname, his Christian name being Giovanni, the Italian form of **John**. It was given to him in his worldly youth because of his love of fashionable French things. It was first used in Britain in the 15th century. *Fran* is a short form along with *Frank* and *Frankie*. Frank can be used as an independent name.

Françoise *see* Frances

Frank, Frankie *see* Frances, Francis

Franklin m.

From medieval English and means 'free'. A franklin was a man who owned land in his own right but was not a noble. A famous modern user was Franklin D. Roosevelt, the 32nd US President.

Fraser, Frazer m.

A Scottish surname of unknown meaning, used as a first name.

Frea see Freya

Fred, Freddie, Freddy see Alfred, Frederick

Freda see Frederick, Winifred

Frederick m. Frederica f.

From the Old German, meaning 'peaceful ruler'. It is also found with such spellings as *Frederic* and *Frederik*. Common abbreviations are *Fred*, *Freddie* and *Freddy*, also used as independent names. The female form is *Frederica*, the origin of the names *Freda*, *Frida* or *Frieda* (the last two influenced by the German form, Friede).

Freya f.

The name of the ancient Norse goddess of beauty,

love and fertility. It can also be found as *Frea* or
spelt the Swedish way *Freja*.

Frida, Frieda *see* Frederick

Fulvia *f.*
Tthe feminine form of a noble Roman family name
meaning 'tawny-haired'. See also **Flavia**.

G

Gabriel *m.*, **Gabrielle** *f.*

From Hebrew, containing the elements 'God', 'man' and 'strength', and possibly implying the phrase 'strong man of God' or 'God is my strength'. In St Luke's Gospel, Gabriel is the Archangel who announces to Mary that she is to bear the baby Jesus. The name has been used infrequently since the Middle Ages for boys. *Gabrielle*, the female form taken from the French, is much more common, along with the Italian *Gabriella*. A short form is *Gaby* and *Abby* is sometimes used.

Gaea *see* **Gaia**

Gaenor *see* **Jennifer**

Gail *f.*
Originally, a pet form of **Abigail**, now widely used

163

as a name in its own right. The spellings *Gale* and *Gayle* are also found.

Gaia *f.*

In Greek myth *Gaea* or Gaia is the earth goddess, the universal mother, probably once the most important divinity. Her name is occasionally found used as a first name, usually with 'green' or feminist overtones.

Gaius *see* Caius

Gale *see* Gail

Gareth *m.*

From the Welsh meaning 'gentle'. This name was used by the 15th-century writer Malory in his *Morte d'Arthur*, and later by Alfred Tennyson, the 19th-century poet, in his version of Malory's story, *Gareth and Lynnette*. It was due to the latter that the name was revived in this century. *Garth* and **Gary** or *Garry* can be used as short forms.

Garfield *m.*

A surname meaning 'spearfield' in Old English, used as a first name, probably after J.A. Garfield (1831-81), 20th president of the USA. The cricketer Sir Garfield (Gary) Sobers is a well-known holder of the name, and also shows its short form.

Garret, Garrett *see* Gerard

Garth, Garry *see* Gareth

Gary *m.*

While this can be used as a short form of both
Gareth and **Garfield**, its use as an independent
name owes much to the film star Gary Cooper
(1901-61). He was born Frank James Cooper, and
chose his stage name from the American town of
Gary. *Garry* is also found, reflecting the usual pronunciation, although Gary Cooper pronounced his
name to rhyme with 'airy'.

Gaspar, Gaspard *see* Jasper

Gaston *m.*

A French name, originally spelt Gascon and meaning a man from the region of Gascony. It is a
common French first name which has been used
occasionally in Britain.

Gavin *m.*

The name of Sir *Gawain*, King Arthur's famous
nephew was Gauvin in Old French, and from
France was adopted in Scotland as Gavin.

Originally confined to Scotland, the name is now found throughout the English-speaking world.

Gay(e) *f.*

This name is simply the adjective meaning happy and lively, and its use dates from this century. Since the adoption of the word 'gay' by the homosexual community, few parents have used the name.

Gayle *see* Gail

Gaynor *see* Jennifer

Gemma *f.*

The Italian word for 'gem'. Its modern use is probably due in part to the Italian saint Gemma Galgani (1875-1903), canonized in 1940. For a long time it was rarely used but, in the 1980s, it became one of the most popular in the country. It is also spelt *Jemma*.

Gene *see* Eugene

Genevieve *f.*

A French name possibly meaning 'lady of the people'. It is found in Latin records as *Genovera* and *Genoveva*. St Genevieve is the patron saint of

Paris; she saved the city from the Huns in the 5th century by her cool thinking, courage and prayer. The name has been used in Britain since the 19th century. French pet forms are **Gina**, *Ginette* and *Veva*.

Geoffrey, Jeffrey m.

From the Old German *Gaufrid* the second half of which means 'peace', but the meaning of the first half is unclear. Geoffrey or Jeffrey was popular between the 12th and 15th centuries in England resulting in many surnames e.g. Jeffries, Jeeves, Jepson. It fell from favour from the 15th until the 19th century, when it was revived. *Geoff* and *Jeff* are common abbreviations.

George m.

From the Greek meaning 'farmer'. The famous St George is said to have been a Roman soldier who was martyred in Palestine in AD 303. In early Christian art many saints were represented as trampling on dragons, as a symbol of good conquering evil. This may be an explanation of how the legend of St George and the dragon originated. In the Middle Ages, St George was closely associated with knighthood and chivalry, and after 1349, when Edward III founded the Order of the

Garter and put it under St George's protection, he became the patron saint of England. Despite this, the name was not much used until the Hanoverian succession in 1714 brought a line of four Georges to the throne. It is currently popular with parents. *Geordie* is a Scottish and North Country pet form which is used as a nickname for Tynesiders.

Georgina *f.*

Georgina and *Georgia* are the most common female forms of **George**, both a popular choice at the moment. They were first used in Britain in the 18th century, when George became popular. The form then was *Georgiana*, which is still sometimes used. Other feminine forms of George are *Georgette* and *Georgine*.

Ger, Gerry *see* Gerald, Gerard

Geraint *m.*

This is a very old Welsh name, a variant form of the Latin Gerontius, which is in turn derived from a Greek word meaning 'old'. The 19th-century poet, Alfred Tennyson used the old Welsh story of Geraint and Enid in his *Idylls of the King*, and it was from this that the name's modern use has stemmed. The real-life hero on which the fictional character is based died in battle in AD 530.

Gerald *m.*

From the Old German, meaning 'spear rule'. It was used in England from the 11th to the 12th century and was probably introduced by the Normans. The name flourished in Ireland due to the influence of the Fitzgerald ('Sons of Gerald') family, the powerful rulers of Kildare. It was probably from Ireland that the name returned to England in the late 19th century. Shortened forms are *Ger*, *Gerry* and *Jerry*.

Geraldine *f.*

Geraldine started life as a poetic nickname used by the 16th-century Earl of Surrey, in a poem praising the beauty of Lady Elizabeth Fitzgerald. Geraldine therefore means 'one of the Fitzgeralds'. It shares short forms with **Gerald**.

Gerard *m.*

From the Old German, meaning 'spear-brave'. It was brought to Britain by Norman settlers and was very common in the Middle Ages. The surnames Gerrard and Garrett are derived from it, and these were the most common medieval pronunciations of the name, although it is not always possible to distinguish between forms of

Gerard and **Gerald**. *Garret(t)* is still used in Ireland. *Ger*, *Gerry* and *Jerry* are used as short forms.

Germaine *f.*

From the Latin word *germanus*, meaning 'brotherly' which was then given a feminine ending. It is more widely used in France than in Britain, although the writer and academic Germaine Greer has made the name widely known in this country.

Gerry *see* Gerald, Geraldine, Gerard

Gertrude *f.*

is from the Old German meaning 'strong spear'. The name came to Britain in the Middle Ages from the Netherlands, where a saint of that name was popular. It was much used in the 19th and earlier 20th centuries, but is not often chosen by parents now. Pet forms are **Gert** or **Gertie**, and *Trudi*, *Trudie* or *Trudy* come from a German pet form of the name.

Gervais, Gervase *m.*

From the Old German, meaning 'spear vassal' or 'armour bearer'. The name was first used among

English churchmen of the 12th century in honour of the 1st-century martyr St Gervase. It spread to the general public, giving rise to the surname Jarvis. Gervais is the French spelling.

Geunor *see* Jennifer

Ghislaine *f.*
This is an Old French name, related to **Giselle** and meaning 'pledge, hostage'. It has only come to be used in this country comparatively recently. It is also found in the forms *Ghislane* and *Ghislain*, although in France this last form is used for boys. It is pronounced with a hard 'g' and the 's' is silent.

Gib *see* Gilbert

Gideon *m.*
From the Hebrew, now generally thought to mean 'having a stump for a hand', although the traditional translation was 'a hewer'. It is the name of an Old Testament Israelite leader who put the forces of the Midianites to flight. The name was adopted at the Reformation and was a favourite among the Puritans who took it to North America where it is still in use.

171

Gigi *f.*

This name became well-known in 1958, when the novel *Gigi* by the French writer Colette was made into a very successful musical film. In the book Gigi is the pet form of Gilberte, the French feminine form of **Gilbert**.

Gilbert *m.*

From the Old German meaning 'bright hostage'. The Normans brought the name to England and it was common in medieval times, when St Gilbert of Sempringham (died 1189) was much admired. Shortened forms are *Gib, Gilly,* **Bert** and *Bertie*.

Giles *m.*

According to legend, St Giles was an Athenian who took his name, Aegidius, from the goatskin that he wore. He left Greece in order to escape the fame of his miracles, and became a hermit in France. There the name became Gilles. The name is first recorded in England in the 12th century, but despite the large number of churches dedicated to the saint, the name was not popular. It has been suggested that this may be because of St Giles's association with beggars and cripples of whom he is the patron saint. However, recent years have seen a marked increase in its popularity. It is sometimes spelt *Gyles*.

Gillian *f.*

This name, which is an English rendering of the Latin name **Juliana**, was so common in the Middle Ages that its short form *Gill* was used as a general term for a girl, as Jack was for a man. It was revived in the 20th century and once again became very popular. A variant form is *Jillian*, and **Jill**, the abbreviated form, is now given as an independent name. *Jilly* is also found.

Gilly *see* Gilbert

Gina *f.*

A short form of such names as **Georgina** and Regina (see **Queenie**), now used as an independent name. In France, Gina and *Ginette* are pet forms of **Genevieve**.

Ginette *see* Genevieve, Gina

Gini, Ginny *see* Virginia

Giselle *f.*

From the Old German meaning a 'pledge' or 'hostage'. *Gisèle* has for a long time been a com-

mon French name, and the English form Giselle
and the latinized *Gisela* have been used in Britain
(see also **Ghislaine**).

Giulia *see* Julia

Giulietta *see* Juliet

Gladys *f.*
This is the anglicized form of *Gwladys*, which
means 'ruler'. It is recorded in Wales as early as
the 5th century, but only moved into the main-
stream of names in the 19th century. In the earlier
part of this century it was very popular, but in
recent decades it has become less fashionable. It
is often shortened to *Glad*.

Glen(n), Glyn(n) *m. and f.*
These are both forms of Celtic words for 'a valley'.
In the last forty years they have become popular
names throughout the English-speaking world.
Glenna is also found for girls.

Glenda *f.*
This is a Welsh name meaning 'holy and good'.

Glenice, Glenis *see* Glenys

Glenn, Glenna *see* **Glen**

Glenys *f.*
From the Welsh meaning 'holy'. It is spelt in a variety of ways, including *Glen(n)is*, *Glennys* and *Glenice* (see also **Glynis**).

Glinys *see* **Glynis**

Gloria *f.*
This is Latin for 'glory' or 'fame'. The name seems to have been coined by George Bernard Shaw (1889) in his play *You Never Can Tell*. It was very common in the first half of the 20th century.

Glyn *see* **Glen**, **Glynis**

Glynis *f.*
From the Welsh for 'a little valley', and thus related to **Glen** and **Glyn**. It can be spelt *Glinys*, and is often confused with **Glenys**.

Glynn *see* **Glen**

Godfrey *m.*
From the Old German meaning 'God's peace'. It was brought to Britain by the Normans.

Gordon m.

This was originally a Scottish place name from which the local lords took their name, which then became the name of a large and famous clan. It was rarely used as a first name until 1885, when the dramatic death of General Gordon at Khartoum gave the name immense popularity.

Grace f.

The vocabulary word, originally used in its religious sense. This name existed as *Gracia*, the Latin form, in the Middle Ages but did not become common until the Puritans adopted Grace along with other Christian qualities as a name. Its popularity waned in the 18th century, but it came back into favour when Grace Darling captured the hearts of the people with her heroic exploit in 1838. With her father, the lighthouse-keeper of the Farne Islands, she rescued nine survivors from a shipwreck in a terrifying storm. The pet form *Gracie*, made famous in Britain in the 20th century by the singer and comedienne, Gracie Fields, is sometimes given as a separate name.

Graham m.

Like Gordon, this was originally a place name

which developed into a family name, particularly on the English/Scottish border. At first restricted to this area, it gradually came into general use as a first name. *Graeme* and *Grahame* are also found.

Grainne, Grania *f.*

In Irish and Scottish legend, Grainne was a princess betrothed to Finn Mac Coul, the famous chieftain. However Grainne preferred **Dermot** and eloped with him. The story of **Finn**'s pursuit of the couple and Grainne's suicide after Finn brought about Dermot's death is an important subject in Irish literature. Grania is the anglicized form of the name, reflecting the prounciation 'grahn-ya'.

Grant *m.*

A surname from the French word meaning 'tall, large' used as a first name. It seems to have come to this country from the USA, where its introduction may have been connected with the popularity of General Ulysses Grant, the 18th President. But since it is a common Scots surname, there is no reason why the name would not have developed independently in this country.

Gregory *m.*

From the Greek meaning 'watchman'. The name

first came to Britain through St Gregory the Great, the pope who sent St Augustine to England. It was in common use from the Norman Conquest, when most Latin names were introduced, until the Reformation when, because of its association with the papacy, it fell out of use. Gregour was the usual medieval form, which is still found as *Gregor* in Scotland, and hence the surname MacGregor. The most common shortened form is *Greg*.

Greta *f.*

A Swedish abbreviation of **Margaret**. It was rare in England until the 20th century, when the fame of the film actress Greta Garbo led to some parents using it. *Gretel* and *Gretchen* are the German forms.

Griffith *m.*

From the Welsh name *Gruffud* or *Gruffydd*, meaning 'lord' or 'strong warrior'. It has always been fairly popular in Wales, and was the name of several Welsh princes. *Griff* is a pet form.

Griselda *f.*

From the Old German, the meaning being disputed but possibly 'grey battle-maiden'. Chaucer told the story of *Patient Griselda* in the *Canterbury Tales*, which encouraged its use by parents who wanted meek and virtuous daughters. *Grizel* is an old Scots form which is little used now, and *Zelda* which has had a mild fashion, started as a short form.

Gruffud, Gruffydd *see* Griffith

Guendolen *see* Gwendolyn

Guenevere, Guinevere *see* Jennifer

Gus, Gussie *see* Augusta

Guy m.

From the Old German, Wido, the meaning of which is uncertain, possibly 'wide' or 'wood'. Wido became Guido in Latin records and Guy was the French form introduced to Britain by the Normans. Apparently the medieval clergy identified the name with the Latin *Vitus* meaning 'lively', hence the disease St Vitus' Dance is known in France as *la danse de Saint Guy*. St Vitus was a Sicilian martyr who was invoked for the cure of nervous ailments. The name fell out of use after Guy Fawkes' gunpowder plot in the 17th century.

It was revived in the 19th century with the help of Walter Scott's novel, *Guy Mannering*, and is quite popular at the moment.

Gwen *f.*
The pet form of several names, such as **Gwendolyn**, which come from the Welsh word meaning 'white'. Gwen and *Gwenda* (a pet form, which can also mean 'fair and good') are now used as separate names and have spread to the rest of Britain.

Gwendolyn, Gwendolen, Guendolen *f.*
From the Welsh meaning 'white circle', probably a reference to the ancient moon-goddess. The name occurs frequently in Welsh legend. Its wide range of spellings also include *Gwendoline* and *Gwendolyne*. It was a popular name at the beginning of the century, but is not much used now.

Gwenfrewi *see* Winifred

Gwenhwyfar *see* Jennifer

Gwill, Gwilym *see* William

Gwladys *see* Gladys

Gwyn *m.*

From the Welsh meaning 'white' or 'blessed'. This name has been anglicized as *Wyn* or *Wynne*. Its use is mainly confined to the Welsh. *Gwynfor* or *Wynfor* is Gwyn with the word for 'great' added to the end.

Gwyneth *f.*

From the Welsh meaning either 'fair maiden' or 'happiness'. *Gwyn* is the pet form.

Gyles *see* Giles

H

Hadrian *see* **Adrian**

Hal *see* **Henry**

Haley *see* **Hayley**

Ham *see* **Abraham**

Hamish *m.*
The anglicized form of Seumas (see **Seamas**), the Gaelic form of **James**. This name became popular in the second half of the 19th century, and is still used, mostly in Scotland.

Hank *see* **Henry**

Hannah *f.*
From the Hebrew meaning 'God has favoured me'. In the Old Testament it was the name of Samuel's mother. The Greek form of this, Anna (see **Anne**),

was used at first. Hannah was only adopted in England after the Reformation. It is currently one of the most popular girl's names.

Harald *see* **Harold**

Harold *m.*

From the Old Norse, meaning 'army-power'; *Harald* is the Scandinavian form. It was used in the Middle Ages, but went out of fashion until the 18th century when it became popular again. Its later popularity stems from 19th-century literature celebrating King Harold II, the last of the Saxon kings, who fought William the Conqueror, and was killed at Hastings in 1066. It is not much used at the moment. It shares the abbreviation *Harry* with **Henry**.

Haroun *see* **Aaron**

Harriet *f.*

A female form of **Henry**, derived from Harry, which was the usual form of the name Henry in the Middle Ages. The name was very popular in the 18th and 19th centuries and has recently been popular again. Short forms are *Hattie* or *Hatty*.

Harrison *m.*

A surname meaning 'son of Harry,' used as a first name. It was popular in the last century and has once again come to be well known thanks to such users as the actor, Harrison Ford.

Harry *see* Harold, Henry

Harun *see* Aaron

Harvey *m.*

From the French meaning 'battle-worthy'. It was common until the 14th century, and had a slight revival in the 19th. Its modern use as a first name may be due in part to its widespread use as a surname.

Hattie, Hatty *see* Harriet

Havelock *see* Oliver

Hayden, Haydon, Haydn *see* Aidan

Hayley *f.*

From a surname meaning 'hay field'. This name came into use in the 1960s, after the success of the film actress, Hayley Mills, and has since become very popular. It is also spelt *Haley* and *Haylie*.

Hazel *f.*
This is one of several plant names adopted as a girl's name in the 19th century.

Heather *f.*
One of the plant names first used in the 19th century. Since heather is a feature of Northern Britain, the name became especially popular in Scotland.

Hector *m.*
From the Greek meaning 'hold fast'. It was the name of the Trojan hero who was killed by the Greek Achilles and took quite a strong hold in Scotland, where it was used as an equivalent for the quite unconnected Gaelic name *Eachan*, which means 'a horseman'.

Heidi *f.*
This name is a pet form of the German version of **Adelaide**. It has come into use in the English-speaking world thanks to the popularity of Johanna Spyri's *Heidi* stories.

Helen *f.*
From the Greek meaning 'the bright one'. The popularity of this name in Britain was due origi-

nally to the 4th-century St *Helena*. She was the mother of Constantine the Great and was supposed to have been the daughter of the ruler of Colchester, the Old King Cole of nursery rhyme. When she was over eighty she made a pilgrimage to the Holy Land where she was believed to have found the true cross of Christ. The name is first found as *Elena* and then **Elaine** and **Ellen**. The 'h' was not used until the Renaissance, when the study of classical literature brought Homer's story of the Trojan war and the beautiful Greek queen Helen to public notice. *Lena* is a contraction of Helena (see also **Eleanor**) and **Nell** a pet form (see also **Ilona**).

Helga *f.*

From the Norse, meaning 'holy'. It has occasionally been used in Britain but is more common in North America, where it was introduced by Scandinavian immigrants (see also **Olga**).

Heloise, Heloïse *see* Eloise

Henri *see* Henry

Henrietta *f.*

The female form of Henry. It was introduced into

this country in the 17th century by Henriette Marie, Charles I's French wife. The full form gave way to the abbreviated Harriet, but was revived in the 19th century. Abbreviations are *Etta*, *Ettie* and *Hetty*.

Henry *m.*

From the Old German, meaning 'home ruler'. The Latin Henricus became *Henri* in France. *Harry* was, in fact, the original English form of Henri, used until the 17th century and often abbreviated to *Hal*. Today, Harry is used as the pet form of Henry and increasingly as a name in its own right. *Hank* is a pet form more common in America.

Herbert *m.*

From the Old German meaning 'bright army'. It seldom appears before the Norman Conquest, after which it became quite common. It was revived at the beginning of the 19th century, and became quite popular again towards the end of the century. This latest revival was partly due to the fashion for adapting aristocratic surnames, but has also been attributed to the popularity of George Herbert's hymns. *Herb*, *Herbie* and **Bert** or *Bertie* are short forms.

Herman *m.*

A Germanic name meaning 'soldier'. The French form of the name is *Armand*, and the old English form *Armin* or *Arminel*, which along with *Arminelle* can also be used as a feminine name.

Hermione *f.*

From the Greek meaning 'daughter of Hermes' and in Greek mythology Hermione was the daughter of Menelaus and **Helen**. Hers is a tragic story, and it was Shakespeare's use of the name in *A Winter's Tale* that gave rise to its use in modern times. He used another form, *Hermia*, in *A Midsummer Night's Dream*, and this has also been found from time to time.

Hester *see* Esther

Hetty *see* Esther, Henrietta

Hew *see* Hugh

Hilary *f.* and *m.*

From the Latin meaning 'cheerful'. The original Latin forms *Hilaria* and *Hilarius* are very occasionally found, and the writer *Hilaire* Belloc used the French form. Hilary, or *Hillary*, was once quite usual as a boy's name, but is now rarely used except for girls.

Hilda *f.*

From the Old English word for 'battle'. There was an Anglo-Saxon St Hilda who was a woman of outstanding ability and who founded an abbey at Whitby in the 7th century. When the names of Anglo-Saxon saints were revived in the 19th century Hilda became popular but is now often felt to be rather old-fashioned.

Hillary *see* Hilary

Hiram *m.*

From the Hebrew, meaning 'brother of the high one', and the name of a king of Tyre in the Old Testament. It was a favourite name in the 17th century and was taken at that time to North America where the name still flourishes.

Hodge *see* Roger

Holly *f.*

The plant name used as a first name. Holly Martins, the hero of Graham Greene's *The Third Man* is a rare example of its use as a man's name.

Honoria *f.*

From the Latin, meaning 'reputation' or 'honour'. The Latin forms **Honora**, Honoria and **An(n)ora** were predominant unil the Reformation, when the Puritans adopted the abstract virtue names and used **Honour** and **Honor**. They were then used both as masculine and feminine names. In the 19th century the Latin forms were revived (see also **Nora**).

Hope *f.*

This Christian virtue was adopted as a first name in the 17th century, in the same way as **Faith** and **Charity**. It was especially popular among Puritans at this time, who used it for both sexes. It is now only used for girls, and is becoming quite popular.

Horace, Horatio *m.*

From the Roman clan named *Horatius* of which the famous **Horatius** who defended the bridge was a member. The fame of the name is also due to the Latin poet Horace. Horatio seems to have come from Italy to England in the 16th century, and has been kept alive by the fame of Nelson, although Horace is the form more likely to be found today. *Horatia* is a rare feminine form.

Howard *m.*

Like other aristocratic family names, this was adopted as a first name by the general public in the 19th century. The origin of the surname is disputed. It may be from the Old German meaning 'heart-protection' or the French for 'worker with a hoe', or even from the medieval official, the 'hogwarden', who superintended the pigs of a district. *Howie* can be used as a short form.

Hubert *m.*

From the Old German meaning 'bright mind'. This name was popular in the Middle Ages, probably as a result of the fame of St Hubert of Liège, the patron saint of huntsmen. It was not much used from the 16th to the 18th centuries, after which it was revived to some extent, but it has since gone out of fashion again. **Bert** is the short form.

Hugh, Hugo *m.*

From the Old German meaning 'heart' or 'soul'. It appears frequently in the Domesday Book. It was further strengthened by the popularity of St Hugh, Bishop of Lincoln in the 14th century. Hugo is the Latin form, and both are quite popular at the moment. *Hew* and *Huw* are Welsh forms of the name; *Hughie* and *Huey* are used as pet forms.

Humphrey *m.*

From the Old German meaning 'peace'. This name was originally spelt with an 'f', the 'ph' coming in when it was equated with the name of the obscure Egyptian saint, Onuphrios, in order to Christianize it. The name appears in the Old English period, and its popularity was reinforced by the Norman Conquest. At first it was confined to the nobility, but later its use became general. As a result of becoming too common, it fell out of favour but was revived in the 19th century.

Hunter *m.*

The Old English vocabulary word used as a first name, and is another surname that has come to be used as a boy's name.

Huw *see* Hugh

Hywel *m.*

A Welsh name meaning 'eminent'. It has become well known through the actor Hywel Bennett.

I

Iain, Ian *see* **John**

Ianthe *f.*

This is an ancient Greek name meaning 'violet flower'. It has a strong literary flavour, having been used by a number of poets including Byron and Shelley. It is still quietly but steadily used.

Ida *f.*

From the Old German, meaning 'hard work'. The name was introduced by the Normans, and lasted until about the middle of the 14th century. In the late 19th century it was revived by Tennyson for the name of the heroine of his poem, *The Princess Ida*, which Gilbert and Sullivan subsequently took as a basis for the operetta *Princess Ida*. These uses led to a revival of the name at the end of the 19th century.

Idris *m.*
This is a Welsh name meaning 'fiery lord'. In Welsh legend, Idris the Giant was an astronomer and magician, who had his observatory on Cader Idris.

Iefan *see* Evan

Iesha *see* Ayesha

Ieuan, Ifan *see* Evan

Ifor *see* Ivor

Ignatius *m.*
Ignatius or *Inigo* is a Latin name, derived originally from a Greek name of obscure origin, possibly meaning 'fiery'. The name took root mainly in Russia and Spain. It was carried further afield by the Jesuits whose founder was Inigo Lopez de Recalde, better known as St Ignatius of Loyola.

Ike *see* Isaac

Ilona *f.*
This is an unusual name, the Hungarian form of Helen.

Imelda *f.*

Imelda is probably the Italian form of the Germanic name Irmhilde 'universal battle'. It is the name of a rather obscure saint, and had a certain popularity in Ireland in the middle of the century.

Imogen *f.*

First appearing in Shakespeare's *Cymbeline*, this name is thought to be a misprint of the name Innogen which appears in Shakespeare's source for the story. It may be derived from the Greek meaning 'beloved child'. It is quite popular at the moment.

Ina *f.*

This name can come from three different sources. It is an Irish form of **Agnes**, a form of the name **Ena**, and can also be a pet form of first names ending '-ina', such as *Christina* and **Georgina**.

India *f.*

This is one of the most recent names to become fashionable. It was the name of a character in *Gone with the Wind*, but its popularity is more likely to be due to the interest, particularly since the 1970s, in Indian culture and religion.

Inés, Inez see Agnes

Ingrid f.

From the Old Norse, meaning 'Ing's ride'. Ing, in Norse mythology, was the god of fertility and crops who rode a golden-bristled boar. The name is common in Scandinavia. The Swedish film star, Ingrid Bergman (1915-82), made the name famous in this country. *Ingeborg* ('Ing's fortress') and *Inga*, the short form of these two names are also found occasionally.

Inigo see Ignatius

Iola f.

The Latin form of a Greek name meaning 'dawn cloud'. In Greek mythology Hercules fell in love with a princess *Iole* . The name is rare in Britain.

Iolanthe see Yolanda

Iona f.

This is the name of the Scottish island used as a first name. The island seems originally to have been called Ioua, 'yew-tree island', but at some point the 'u' was misread as 'n' and so the island got its present name. The name's popularity has been increasing in recent years. *Ione* ('eye-oh-nee') is not the same name, but a Greek name connected with the word 'violet'.

Ior *see* Ivor

Ira *m.*
A name from the Old Testament meaning 'watchful'. The name was used by the Puritans, who took it over to America where it is now much more common than in Britain. The song writer Ira Gershwin was a famous bearer of the name.

Irene *f.*
The name of the goddess of peace and also of one of the seasons in ancient Greece. Although the name was used earlier in other parts of Europe, it was not used in England until the late 19th century. It is now very common. The abbreviation *Renie* is sometimes used and it can also be found in the form *Irena*. Irene is pronounced in two different ways: in the Greek way with three syllables and the final 'e' pronounced, and the usual modern way with only two syllables.

Iris *f.*
Although this name is usually associated with the

flower, it comes from the Greek word for 'rainbow', after which the flower was named because of its bright colours. In Greek mythology Iris carried messages from the gods to men, across the rainbow which was her bridge. It was not used in England before the 19th century.

Irma *f.*

This was originally a German name meaning 'universal'. It has only been used in this country since the beginning of the last century.

Irving *m.*

Irving or *Irvine* are Scottish place names which were used first as surnames and then as first names.

Isa *see* Isabel

Isaac *m.*

From the Hebrew meaning 'laughter'. It was the name given by Sarah, wife of Abraham, to the son born in her old age. The name is popularly believed to have been chosen by Sarah because she laughed when she was told that she would conceive. The name appears in Britain in the Middle Ages, but it came to be regarded as a specifically Jewish name. The name came into general use in the 16th and 17th centuries, when it was spelt with a 'z' as in *Izaak* Walton, the author of *The Compleat Angler*. In the mid-17th century the 's' spelling came into fashion, as in Sir Isaac Newton, the great scientist. *Zak* or **Ike** are used as pet forms.

Isabel(le), Isobel *f.*

These are variant forms of **Elizabeth** which developed in medieval France. Elizabeth became Ilsabeth and then Isabeau, and finally *Isabelle*. Up to the end of the 17th century at least, the derivatives *Isabel(le)* in England, Isobel in Scotland and the Gaelic *Iseabail*, sometimes spelt phonetically as *Ishbel*, were interchangeable with Elizabeth. *Isa* and *Bel(le)* were the common short forms. The Latin *Isabella* and *Bella* were used from the 18th century. Of the three spellings Isabel seems to be the most popular at the moment, followed by Isobel, but all forms of the name are much used, and can also occur in such forms as *Ysabel*.

Isadora *see* Isidore

Isaiah *m.*

From the Hebrew meaning 'Jehovah is salvation',

199

and the name of the great Old Testament prophet. It was first used by the 17th-century Puritans and is rather rare today in Britain, although slightly more common in North America. The philosopher Sir Isaiah Berlin is a famous modern holder of the name.

Iseabail *see* Isabel

Iseult *see* Isolda

Ishbel *see* Isabel

Isidore *m.*, Isidora *f.*
From the Greek, possibly meaning 'gift of Isis'. There were two Spanish saints of this name. The scandal caused by the private life and dancing style of *Isadora* Duncan (1878-1927) made the feminine form of the name well known.

Isla *f.*
A Scottish island name, used as a girl's name in Scotland since the 1950s. It has now spread to other parts of the country. The 's' is silent, as in 'island'.

Isleen *see* Aisling

Isobel *see* Isabel

Isolda *f.*

From Old Welsh **Essylt** meaning 'fair one'. It was a common name in medieval times because of its place in the tragic legend of **Tristan** and Isolda. **Iseult** was the Norman form which became Isolda in Latin, Isot(t) in Middle English. Isolda or **Isolde** had a brief revival in the 19th century owing to the popularity of Wagner's opera *Tristan and Isolde*. It is also spelt **Yseult(e)** and **Ysolde**.

Israel *f.*

From Hebrew, although its meaning is disputed; the most likely translation is 'may God prevail'. In the Old Testament Jacob was named Israel after his struggle with the angel of God. The name was first adopted by Christians after the Reformation. It continued in use until the late 19th century, but is now uncommon.

Ivan *m.*

The Russian form of **John**, found occasionally in Britain.

Ivo *m.*

From the Old German meaning 'yew'. It was common in Brittany in the form *Yves*, and was brought to Britain at the time of the Norman Conquest. It has been used occasionally since.

Ivor, Ifor *m.*

Ifor is a Welsh name which means 'lord', and Ivor is the anglicized spelling. It was originally *Ior*, but was probably influenced by the Breton version, *Yves*, which became **Ivo** and was brought over by the Normans.

Ivy *f.*

This is a plant name which came into use in the 19th century. Because ivy clings so firmly, the name may have been used to indicate faithfulness.

Izaak *see* Isaac

J

Jacaline *see* **Jacqueline**

Jack *m.*

Originally the pet form of **John**, this is now a
popular name in its own right. In the Middle Ages
Jan evolved from John, and then developed the pet
form Jankin. This in turn lost its middle 'n' and
final 'in' to give Jack. *Jock* is a traditionally Scottish
form. Jack shares the pet form *Jake*, now a name
in its own right, with **Jacob**.

Jackalyn, Jackie, Jacky *see* **Jacqueline**

Jacob *m.*

The meaning of this Hebrew name is uncertain. In
the Old Testament, it was the name of Isaac's
younger son, who tricked his brother Esau out of
his inheritance. This explains the popular interpretation of the name as 'he supplanted'. There were

two Latin forms, *Jacobus* and *Jacomus*. Jacob came from the former and **James** from the latter. Jacob has survived as a first name because translators of the Bible kept this form for the Old Testament Patriarch, although they called the two New Testament apostles James. *Jacoba*, *Jacobine* and *Jacobina* are rare feminine forms. *Jake* is an abbreviation shared with **Jack** and now used as a name in its own right.

Jacqueline *f.*

Jacqueline and *Jacquetta* are French feminines of *Jacques*, the French equivalent of **James** and **Jacob**. Both were introduced into this country in the 13th century, and have been in use ever since. Jacqueline, with its pet forms *Jacky*, *Jackie* or *Jacqui*, is found in a very wide range of spellings which include *Jackalyn*, *Jacaline*, *Jacquelyn* and *Jaqueline*.

Jade *f.*

The name of the precious stone used as a first name. Although the names of precious stones have been in use as girls' names since the last century, this one seems only to have come into use in the 1970s.

Jake *see* **Jack, Jacob, Jesse**

Jamal *see* **Jamila**

James *m.*

This name has the same root as **Jacob**. It became established in Britain in the 12th century when pilgrims started to visit the shrine of St James at Compostella in Spain. At that time the name was more common in Scotland. With the accession of James VI as the first king of both England and Scotland in the 1603, the name became more popular in England. It was unfashionable in the 19th century, but is now probably the most used boy's name. The pet forms are *Jim*, *Jimmy* and **Jamie**. The Irish form is **Seamas** and the Scots **Hamish**.

Jamie *m. and f.*

This pet form of **James** was originally a Scottish form but has since spread throughout the English-speaking world and become popular in its own right. Since at least the 1960s it has also been used as a girl's name, particularly in the United States.

Jamila *f.*

An Arabic name meaning 'beautiful'. It, along with

the boy's form, *Jamal,* has been popular in the USA with Black Muslims. It is also used in France, where it can be found as *Djamila*.

Jan *f. and m.*

The female version is a common pet form of **Janet**. The male form is a form of **John** in a number of European languages such as Dutch and Polish and is then pronounced *yan*. It is also the old English pronunciation of John, still used in the West Country.

Jane *f.*

This is now the commonest female form of **John**. It comes from the Old French form Jehane. It was very rare before the 16th century, the medieval female forms of John being **Joan** and **Joanna**. An early example was Jane Seymour, Henry VIII's third wife, and mother of Edward VI. Since Tudor times the name has been in and out of fashion. At the moment it is freely used as a second name, but rarely as a first unless in some combination like Sarah Jane. It can also be spelt *Jayne*. The commonest pet forms are *Jenny* and *Janey* or *Janie* (see also **Janet**). *Jancis* seems to be a combination of Jane with Frances or Cicely. Other elaborations of the name include *Janice* or *Janis*; *Jana*, a form found in a variety of other languages, and *Janelle* (see also **Sheena**, **Sian**).

Janene *see* Janine

Janet *f.*

This was originally derived from *Jeanette*, the French pet form of **Jean**. It was first used in Scotland. *Janette* and *Janetta* are also found, and **Net**, **Nettie**, **Netta** and **Jan** are pet names. A Scottish pet form is **Jessie** (see also **Sheena**).

Janey, Janice, Janie, Janis *see* Jane

Janine *f.*

Like **Janet**, this name comes from a pet form of *Jeanne*, the French form of **Jean**. It is also spelt *Jannine* and *Janene*, and the latinized *Janina* is also used.

Jaqueline *see* Jacqueline

Jared *m.*

A biblical name meaning 'to descend' and connected with **Jordan**. It was used in the past by the Puritans but had become very rare until the mid-1960s when it became popular in the United States and Australia. It is also found in the forms

Jarred, *Jarod* and *Jarrod*, although some of these forms may be influenced by similar surnames.

Jasmine *f.*
A flower name also found in its normal botanical form, *Jasmin*. The word comes from Persian, and the name is also used in the Persian form *Yasmin*, with variants such as *Yasmine* and *Yasmina*.

Jason *m.*
This name was adopted in the 17th century when biblical names became popular, because it is the traditional name for the author of *Ecclesiasticus*. It has been a popular name in recent years, when parents probably associated it more with the Greek hero Jason, who won the Golden Fleece.

Jasper *m.*
Gaspar or *Caspar* (**Kaspar**) is the traditional name of one of the three kings or wise men of the Christmas story. His name may mean 'keeper' or 'bringer of treasure'. *Gaspard* is the French form and Jasper the English.

Jay *m. and f.*
This name derives most probably from a short form of any name beginning with a 'j', but it could

also be from a surname, originally a nickname referring to the bird and the noise it makes, indicating that the holder was a chatterer. It is sometimes spelt *Jaye*.

Jayne *see* Jane

Jean *f.*
This name started as a Scottish form of **Jane** or **Joan** derived from the Old French Jehane. The diminutive *Jeanette* is also found (see **Janet**). The commonest pet forms are *Jeanie* and *Jenny*.

Jeanette *see* Janet, Jean

Jeanie *see* Jean

Jed *m.*
A short form of the Biblical name *Jedidiah*, which means 'beloved of the Lord'. It is much more common in the United States than in this country.

Jeff, Jeffrey *see* Geoffrey

Jem *see* Jeremy

Jemima *f.*
From the Hebrew meaning 'dove' or 'handsome as

the day', and the name of one of Job's daughters in the Old Testament. It was first used in the 17th century by Puritans, and was very popular in the 19th century and is used steadily today. *Mima* is a pet form.

Jemma *see* Gemma

Jennifer *f.*

Jennifer was an old Cornish form of *Guenevere*, from the Welsh meaning 'white ghost', and the name of King Arthur's wife. It was practically obsolete when it was revived in the 20th century. It spread rapidly, and was very popular in the 1950s and 60s. *Jenny* or *Jenni* is the pet form, shared with **Janet** and **Jane**. *Gaenor*, *Geunor* and *Gaynor* are other forms of Guenevere, which is also spelt *Guinevere* and in Wales, *Gwenhwyfar*. *Jenna*, another Cornish version of the name, has recently become more popular.

Jenny *see* Jane, Jean, Jennifer

Jeremy *m.*

From the Hebrew, meaning 'may Jehovah exalt'. *Jeremiah* was the Old Testament prophet who wrote the *Book of Lamentations*. The traditional

English form is Jeremy, which appears from the 13th century onwards, although in the 17th century, the two forms *Jeremias* and Jeremiah were more common. *Jerry* is a short form, which is shared with **Gerald**, and *Jem* is also used.

Jerome *m.*

From the Greek *Hieronymos*, meaning 'holy name'. This name is pre-Christian in origin, but soon became popular with the early Church. St Jerome translated the Bible into Latin in the 4th century, and was an important religious influence in the Middle Ages. The name appears in England in the 12th century as Geronimus, which gradually gave way to the French form Jerome.

Jerry *see* **Gerald, Geraldine, Gerard, Jeremy**

Jess *see* **Jesse, Jessica**

Jesse *m.*

From the Hebrew meaning 'God exists', and in the Old Testament, the name of King David's father. It was adopted in the 17th century by the Puritans who took it to America where it has been commoner than in this country. Jesse James, the American outlaw, and the politician Jesse Jackson

211

are probably the best known examples. *Jess* is a short form, and *Jake* a pet form shared with **Jacob**. The name is sometimes spelt **Jessie**.

Jessica *f.*

The source of this name is much debated, but it may well have been invented by Shakespeare for his play *The Merchant of Venice* in which Shylock's daughter is called Jessica. It is shortened to *Jess* or **Jessie**, which is sometimes spelt *Jessye*.

Jessie *f.*

This is a Scottish diminutive of **Janet** but is often used as a separate name. It is fairly common in the literature of the 18th and 19th centuries, and is also a pet form of **Jessica** (see also **Jessie**).

Jessye *see* **Jessica**

Jethro *m.*

From the Hebrew meaning 'abundance' or 'excellence'. In the Bible it is the name of **Moses**'s father-in-law. It has been used as a first name since the Reformation, and is now familiar to many from a character in the popular BBC radio serial, *The Archers*, and from the pop group Jethro Tull, named after an 18th-century agriculturalist.

Jill *f.*

A pet form of *Jillian* or **Gillian**, often given as a separate name (see **Julian**).

Jillian, Jilly *see* Gillian, Juliana

Jim, Jimmy *see* James

Jinny *see* Virginia

Jo *see* Joseph, Josephine

Joan *f.*

This is the oldest female form of **John** and is a contraction of Johanna, the Latin feminine form of *Johannes*. The name came over from France as Jhone and Johan in the second half of the 12th century, but by the 14th century Joan was the established form. By the mid-16th century it was so common that it became unfashionable, and **Jane** superseded it. It was revived at the beginning of the 20th century. *Joni* is the pet form.

Joanna, Joanne *f.*

Johanna was the medieval Latin female form of *Johannes* (see **John**), which appears as Joanna in the New Testament (Luke XXIV, 10), as one of the three women who hears the first news of Christ's resurrection. Joanne was a later development of the name. *Juanita* is the Spanish diminutive, which, with its short form *Nita* is also found in Britain.

Job *m.*

From the Hebrew meaning 'hated' or 'persecuted'. *Jobey*, *Jobie* or *Joby* are pet forms of the name.

Jocelyn, Jo(s)celin *m. and f.*

These names seem to be derived from several different names which have come together over a period of time to form one name. The most important source is probably from the Latin meaning 'cheerful, sportive'. There is also a possibility that it is derived from an Old German name meaning 'little Goth'. A further derivation has been traced from the name *Josse*, 'champion', a form of *Jodoc*, the name of an early Breton saint which also gave us **Joyce**. Jocelyn is the normal form for boys, while all forms are used for girls.

Jock *see* Jack

Jodie, Jody *see* Judith

Jodoc *see* **Jocelyn**

Joe *see* **Joseph, Josephine**

Joel *m.*

From the Hebrew, meaning 'Jehovah is God' and the name of one of the minor Old Testament prophets. It was adopted by the Puritans, like many other biblical names, after the Reformation. *Joelle* is a form of the name for girls.

Johan *see* **John**

Johanna *see* **Joanna**

John *m.*

From the Hebrew, meaning 'the Lord is gracious'. Its earliest form in Europe was the Latin *Johannes*, which was shortened to *Johan* and *Jon* before becoming John. However, in France the name became Jean, and both forms of the name were introduced into the British Isles, which resulted in two groups of names developing. Thus the Johannes-form gives us the Gaelic *Ian* and *Iain*, *Ieuan* and **Evan** in Welsh, and *Eoin* ('oh-n) in Irish, while the Jean-form gives **Sean** or **Shane** in Irish and *Sion* in Welsh. Since the 16th century,

John has been one of the commonest boys' names in Britain, although currently used far more often for a second name than a first (see also **Ivan**, **Jack**).

Joisse *see* Joyce

Jolyon *see* Julian

Jon *see* John, Jonathan

Jonah, Jonas *m.*

From the Hebrew meaning 'dove'. The Old Testament story of Jonah and the whale was very popular in the Middle Ages and because of this the name was common. It continued to be used occasionally until the 19th century, when it became rare probably because of the association of the name with bad luck. Jonas is the Greek form of the name and is now the more common of the two.

Jonathan *m.*

A Hebrew name meaning 'the Lord has given'. In the Old Testament, Jonathan was the son of King Saul and it was his great friendship with David that gave rise to the expression 'David and Jonathan' to describe two close friends. The name came into use at the time of the Reformation, and it is popular today. The short form, *Jon*, is often used as a separate name.

Joni *see* Joan

Jordan *m. and f.*
Jordan was quite a popular name in the Middle Ages when it was given to children baptised with water from the River Jordan brought back by pilgrims to the Holy Land. It has recently been revived as a first name, and is given about equally to boys and girls. The name of the river means 'to descend or flow' and comes from the same word that gives us the name **Jared**.

Jos *see* Joseph, Josiah

Joscelin *see* Jocelyn

Joseph *m.*
From the Hebrew meaning 'the Lord added' (i.e. to the family). In the Old Testament it was the name of Jacob and Rachel's elder son who was sold into slavery in Egypt. In the New Testament, there are Joseph, the husband of Mary, and Joseph of Arimathea, who is believed to have buried Jesus

and whom legend connects with Glastonbury and the Holy Grail. The name was not often used until the 17th century, when Old Testament names were adopted by the Puritans, and Joseph became a favourite. *Joe* and *Jo* are common abbreviations, and *Jos* is also found.

Josephine *f.*

Josephine is the French female form of **Joseph**. It was Napoleon's first wife, the Empress Josephine, who started the fashion for the name in Britain and France. *Josepha* and *Josephina* are less common forms of the name. Pet forms are *Jo(e)* and *Josie* and in France, Josephine has the pet form *Fifi*.

Joshua *m.*

From the Hebrew meaning 'the Lord saves'. In the Old Testament Joshua succeeded Moses and finally led the Israelites to the Promised Land. The name was not used in England before the Reformation. *Josh* is a short form. Joshua is quite a popular name at the moment.

Josiah *m.*

From the Hebrew meaning 'may the Lord heal'. It was most common in the 17th century. The 18th-century potter, Josiah Wedgewood, in whose family the name is still used, is possibly the best known British bearer of the name. *Josias* is an alternative form of the name, and *Jos* a short form.

Josie *see* **Josephine**

Josse *see* **Jocelyn, Joyce**

Joy *f.*

This is the vocabulary word used as a first name. It occurs as early as the 12th century but then disappears, to be revived in the 19th century.

Joyce *m. and f.*

In the Middle Ages when this name was most common it usually had the form *Josse*. A 7th-century saint from Brittany, who also gave us the name **Jocelyn**, was the cause of the name's popularity. One of the French variants of the name was *Joisse*, and it was from this that the final form of the name was derived. The name was little used after the Middle Ages until the general revival of medieval names in the last century. It is now very rare as a man's name.

Juanita *see* **Joanna**

Jude *m*.

The Hebrew form of this name is **Yehudi**, which was rendered as **Judah** in the Authorised Version of the Old Testament. **Judas** Iscariot bore the Greek form, and because of him Jude was not used by Christians until the Reformation. The name is still used occasionally, but is best known through Thomas Hardy's novel *Jude the Obscure* and the Beatles' song *Hey Jude*. It means 'praise'.

Judith *f*.

From the Hebrew meaning 'a Jewess', and in the Apocryphal *Book of Judith* the name of the resourceful woman who saves the Israelites by letting the enemy general think he was seducing her, and then once in his tent, cutting off his head with his own sword. The name appears both before and after the Norman Conquest, but did not become common until the 17th century. The short form **Judy** is often given independently, as are the pet forms, **Jody** or **Jodi(e)**.

Jules *see* Julian

Julia *f*.

Julia is the feminine form of **Julius**, which came to England from Italy as **Giulia** in the 16th century. It did not become common in Britain until the 18th and 19th centuries. *Julie* is the French form. Julia was popular in the middle of this century, then fell out of favour, but is now coming back into use.

Julian *m.*

Julianus was a Roman family name which meant 'connected with the family of *Julius*'. Julius probably comes from the same root that gives the Latin word for 'god', but in Roman times the family believed that it referred to the soft growth of hair that forms a boy's first sign of a beard, as this was the state of development that a founding member of the clan had reached when he first distinguished himself in battle. The most famous of numerous saints of this name was St Julian the Hospitaller, who devoted himself to helping poor travellers. The name came to Britain in the Latin form, which was anglicized as *Julyan*, and in the North of England as *Jolyon*. It was popular in the 19th century, and today is quite a common name. Jolyon was used by John Galsworthy in his *Forsyte Saga* novels. *Jules*, the French form of Julius, is also used as a short form of Julian.

Juliana *f.*

This is the feminine form of **Julian**. It was a popular name in the Middle Ages, when the name normally took the form Julian, still occasionally found used for girls. The variant forms **Gillian** and **Jill** were among the commonest girls' names from the 12th to the 15th centuries. The name subsequently dropped out of use but was revived in the 18th century. The short form *Julie* is shared with **Julia** (see also **Lianne**).

Julie *see* **Julia, Juliana**

Juliet *f.*
This is a short form of the Italian *Giulietta*, the diminutive of **Julia**. Its use nowadays is probably the result of the influence of Shakespeare's *Romeo and Juliet. Juliette* is a French form sometimes used in Britain.

Julius, Julias *see* **Julian**

Julyan *see* **Julian**

June *f.*
This is simply the name of the month which, like April, has been used as a girl's name in the 20th century.

Juno *see* **Una**

Justin *m.*, **Justine** *f.*

From the Latin meaning 'just'. These were uncommon names until thirty years ago when they came back into fashion. *Justina* is an old feminine form.

K

Kai *see* **Kay, Caius**

Kane *m.*
This is an Irish surname meaning 'fighter' used as a first name. It has been used more in the USA and Australia than in Great Britain.

Karan *see* **Karen**

Karel *see* **Carol**

Karen *f.*
A Scandinavian form of **Katherine** which was only introduced into this country in the 1930s. Variants include *Karan* and *Karin, Karyn, Caryn, Caron* and *Karyna,* although some of these could be analysed as belonging to **Cara** (see also **Keren**).

Karenza *see* **Kerensa**

Karin *see* **Karen**

Karl, Karla *see* **Carl**

Karyn, Karyna *see* **Karen**

Kasia *see* **Kezia(h)**

Kasimir, Kasimira *see* **Casey**

Kaspar *see* **Jasper**

Katharine, Katherine, Catharine, Catherine *f.*
A name of unknown meaning, but from an early
date associated with the Greek *katharos* meaning
'pure'. The name came to England in the early
12th century when crusaders brought back the
legend of St Katharine of Alexandria. She was an
Egyptian princess who was tortured and put to
death in the early 4th century for her learned
defence of Christianity. The legend and the name
became very popular in Britain, and while its
popularity may fluctuate, it has a long history as
one of the commonest of all girls' names. There
are a number of further spellings for the name, of
which *Kathryn* is one of the most frequent. The
most common short forms are *Kate, Kitty, Katie,
Cathy* and **Kay**, all of which are used as indepen-

dent names. The Irish forms, *Kathleen* or
Cathleen, are now used throughout Britain, while
Caitlin is an older Irish form which has recently
had a revival. *Kathlyn* is a variant of Kathleen.
Russian *Katarina*, *Katia* or *Katya* and *Katinka* are
occasionally found (see also **Catriona**, **Karen**).

Katrina, Katrine *see* Catriona

Katya *see* Katharine

Kay *f. and m.*
A pet form of names beginning with a 'k', such as
Katharine. It has been used as a first name for the
last hundred years, and can also be spelt *Kai* and
Kaye (see also **Caius**).

Kayleigh *f.*
This girl's name suddenly became popular in the
1980s, although it had been around for some years
before then. It is also spelt in forms such as *Kayley*
and *Kaylee*. While it can be interpreted as from an
Irish surname, it is more likely to be a modern creation, used at a time when **Lee** was popular, as
were a number of similar- sounding names
beginning with 'k' such as **Kylie** and **Kelly**. *Keeley*
is either a variation of this name or of Kelly.

Keir *m.*

Keir is a Scottish surname used as a first name. It came into use out of respect for James Keir Hardie (1856-1915), who was generally referred to as Keir Hardie, the first man to be elected as a Labour MP.

Keiran *see* Kieran

Keith *m.*

This is a first name from Scotland which has spread throughout Britain. It was originally a surname taken from the Scottish place name, probably from the Gaelic for 'wood' or 'windy place'.

Kelly *f. and m.*

A modern first name which has rapidly become very popular. It is an Irish surname which means 'warlike' used as a first name. At first mainly a boy's name, it is now more usual for girls. *Kelley* is also found (see also **Kayleigh**, **Kylie**).

Kelvin *m.*

This is the name of the river which flows through Glasgow, used as a first name. The river's name possibly means 'narrow water'.

Kenneth *m.*

This is the English form of the Gaelic *Coinneach*, meaning 'handsome', and equivalent to modern Welsh *Cenydd*. This is basically a Scottish name which became popular when Kenneth MacAlpine became first King of Scotland in the 9th century, uniting the Picts and the Scots. From Scotland it gradually spread over Britain. It is often shortened to *Ken* or *Kenny*.

Kent *m.*

This is the surname taken from the English county used as a first name. It first became popular in the United States. The county name is a ancient one, meaning 'border' from its position on the coast.

Kentigern *see* Mungo

Kenton *m.*

This is taken from a surname, itself from a common place name meaning 'royal manor', and now used as a first name.

Keren *f.*

Although some modern uses of this may be as a form of **Karen**, this is an ancient name, a short form of the Old Testament *Kerenhappuch*, one of the beautiful daughters of **Job**. The name means 'horn (container) of kohl'. It has also been found in the form *Kerena*.

Kerensa, Kerenza *f.*

A Cornish name meaning 'affection, love'. It is also found in the form **Karenza**.

Keri *see* **Ceri**

Kerry *m. and f.*

The Irish county name used as a given name. It is a modern name, apparently first used in Australia usually for boys, but it is now in general use, mainly for girls. It is also found as *Kerri*. Its spread may have been helped by the Welsh name **Ceri**, pronounced in the same way.

Keshia *see* **Kezia**

Kester *see* **Christopher**

Kevin *m.*

From the Irish meaning 'handsome birth'. This name was very popular in Ireland on account of St Kevin, a 6th-century hermit, who later became abbot of Glendalough. It is now widely used throughout the English-speaking world.

Kezia(h) *f.*

The Hebrew word for the spice cassia, and the
name of one of the beautiful daughters of **Job** in
the Bible. The form *Keshia* also occurs, and short
forms of the name are *Kezie*, *Kizzie* and *Kissie* or
Kissy. *Cassia* and *Kasia* have also been recorded,
with the latter also a Polish pet form of **Katharine**.

Kieran *m.*

This is a form of the Irish name *Ciaran*, meaning
'dark-haired'. It was the name of 26 Irish saints
and in the last two or three decades it has become
increasingly popular. It is sometimes spelt *Cieran*,
Keiran or *Kieron*. *Ciara*, *Ciera*, *Kiara* and *Kiera*
are used for girls.

Kim *m. and. f.*

Probably from Old English *cynebeald*, meaning
'royally bold', developing through the surname
Kimball. Rudyard Kipling's hero in the novel *Kim*
(1901) used a shortened form of his true name,
Kimball O'Hara, showing the use of the surname
as a first name. More recently the name has been
commoner for girls. *Kym* is also found.

Kimberl(e)y *f.*

This is another possible source of the name **Kim**.

Kimberley is a diamond-mining town in South Africa, and the association with jewels seems to have encouraged its use. Since it began to be used in the 1940s it has spread rapidly. There was also a brief fashion for Kimberley as a boy's name at the turn of the century, no doubt commemorating events of the Boer War, but this soon died out.

Kirk *m.*

A Scandinavian name meaning 'church', brought to prominence as a first name by the actor, Kirk Douglas. It would originally have been a surname given to someone connected with the church, or who lived near one.

Kirsty, Kirsten *f.*

These are both forms of the name **Christine**. Kirsty was originally a Scottish pet form, while Kirsten comes from Scandinavia. *Kirstin* is also found.

Kissie, Kissy *see* Kezia(h)

Kit *see* Christopher

Kitty *see* Katharine

Kizzie *see* Kezia(h)

Klaus *see* **Nicholas**

Kodey, Kody *see* **Cody**

Korey, Korrie, Kory *see* **Corey**

Krista, Kristin, Kristina, Kryssa, Krystyna *see* **Christine**

Krystal *see* **Crystal**

Kurt *see* **Conrad**

Kyle *m. and f.*
This is a Scottish place and surname meaning 'a strip of land'. It is more usual as a name for boys than girls.

Kylie *f.*
It has been claimed that this Australian name comes from an Aborigine word meaning 'a curl', but it is more probably a modern invention, either a female form of **Kyle** or as a variation on such names as **Kelly**. It is best known in this country through the actress and singer, Kylie Minogue (see also **Kayleigh**).

Kym *see* **Kim**

L

Lachlan *m.*
From Gaelic *Lachlann* or *Lochlann*. This is primarily a Highland name, introduced as a term for the Viking settlers there, but it was taken to Australia and Canada by Scots emigrants and has flourished there. Short forms are *Lachie* or *Lochie* and there is an occasional feminine form *Lachina*.

Laeta, Laetitia *see* Letitia

Laila *see* Leila

Lalage *f.*
From the Latin, meaning 'one who prattles'. Short forms are *Lal* and *Lally*.

Lana *see* Alan

Lancelot *m.*
This is a name of disputed meaning, but possibly

comes from the Old French for a servant. It can also be spelt *Launcelot*, and was used in Britain from the 13th century. This was due to the popularity of Sir Lancelot, the knight without equal, in the stories of King Arthur. The name is more often found today in its short form *Lance*.

Lara *f.*

This is a short form of the Russian name *Larissa*, the meaning of which is uncertain, although it may well be used by some parents as a variation of **Laura**. Lara came into general use in the 1960s after the success of the film of Pasternak's *Dr Zhivago*, with its tragic heroine of this name.

Laraine *see* Lorraine

Larissa *see* Lara

Larrie, Larry *see* Laurence

Latasha, Latisha, Latoya *f.*

There is a strong tradition of name-creating among certain sections of American society, which goes back to at least the last century. These three names are among the commonest of a large group of names which have grown up in the

American black community in the last thirty to forty years. They are mostly blends, that is, combinations of syllables taken from different names, which work because they sound right at the time, echoing the sounds from other popular names (although this leaves Latoya as something of a mystery). Many of these names start with 'La', and particularly 'Lat'. Since names such as *Laverne* (with the option of *Leverne* for boys) were popular with an earlier generation, it may be that the French influence found in place and surnames in the southern USA is the source of this element, although it could just as well come from the many girls' names which begin with these letters.

Launcelot *see* Lancelot

Laura *f.*

Laura is derived, like *Laurel*, from the Latin for 'laurel', a symbol in the classical world of victory and poetic genius. *Lauretta* is the diminutive form. Together with *Laurencia* and *Lora* these names were common from the 12th century. *Lauren* or *Loren* (also used for boys) *Lora* and *Lori* are popular variants of the name. Other diminutives which are sometimes used are *Laureen, Laurene,* and *Laurissa*, *Loretta* and *Lolly*. Laurel, the plant name, sometimes spelt *Lorel*, is also found (see also **Lara**).

Lauraine *see* Lorraine

Laurel *see* Laura

Lauren *see* Laura

Laurence, Lawrence m.
From the Latin meaning 'of Laurentium', a town which took its name from the laurel plant, symbol of victory. It became common in the 12th century. St Laurence, the 3rd-century Archdeacon of Rome, was a favourite medieval saint. It was popular in Ireland because of St Laurence O'Toole, a 12th-century Archbishop of Dublin, whose real name was *Lorcan* (Irish for 'fierce'). *Larrie* or *Larry* is the usual abbreviation in England, while *Laurie* or *Lawrie* is used in Scotland. *Loren* is a form of the name used for both boys and girls.

Laurencia, Laureen, Laurene, Lauretta, Laurissa *see* Laura

Laurie *see* Laurence

Laverne *see* **Latasha**

Lavinia *f.*
The meaning of this name is unknown, but in classical legend it was the name of Aeneas' wife, for whose hand in marriage he fought and defeated a rival suitor. The town of Lavinium, originally called Latium, was renamed after her. The name was very popular for a while during the Renaissance, but then faded out, only returning to fashion in the 18th century. *Lavina* is probably a variant.

Lawrence, Lawrie *see* **Laurence**

Lea *see* **Leah, Lee, Leo**

Leah *f.*
A Hebrew name, probably meaning 'cow'. In the Bible, Leah was the sister of Rachel, and the first wife of Jacob. *Lea* or *Lia*, the Italian form of the name, are sometimes used, although they can also be a short form of a number of names ending in the sound.

Leanne *see* **Lianne**

Leanora, Leanore *see* **Leonora**

Lee, Leigh, Lea *m. and f.*
From the various forms of the surname meaning
'meadow'. The name may have spread from the
southern United States, and its popularity there
probably owes something to the Confederate
general, Robert E. Lee (1807-70). See also
Kayleigh.

Leigh Ann *see* **Lianne**

Leila *f.*
A Persian name meaning 'night', probably indicating 'dark-haired'. Lord Byron started the fashion
for it in the 19th century by using it in a poem with
an oriental setting called *The Giaour*. The name
also appears in the Persian romantic legend of
Leilah and Mejnoun, the Persian equivalent of the
Greek story of Cupid and Psyche. *Laila* is also
used.

Len *see* **Leonard**

Lena *see* **Helen**

Lennie, Lenny, Lennard *see* **Leonard**

Lenore *see* **Leonora**

Leo *m.*, **Leonie** *f.*
From the Latin for 'lion'. Leo was the name of six emperors of Constantinople and of thirteen popes. The name of the politician, *Leon* Brittan, shows its French form, from which the feminine *Leonie* comes. Other versions of the name used for girls include *Lea*, *Leola*, *Leona* and *Leontine*.

Leolin, Leoline *see* **Llewelyn**

Leon *see* **Leo, Lionel**

Leona *see* **Leo**

Leonard *m.*
From the Old German meaning 'brave as a lion'. The 6th-century St Leonhard was a Frankish nobleman who was converted to Christianity. He became a hermit and devoted his life to helping prisoners, of whom he is the patron saint. His popularity made the name common in medieval England and France and the name was revived in the 19th century. The usual shortened forms are *Len*, *Lennie* and *Lenny*. It is sometimes spelt *Lennard*.

239

Leonie *see* Leo

Leonora, Lenore, Leonore *f.*

These names are European forms of **Eleanor**, all of which have been used from time to time in this country. None of them appeared in Britain before the 19th century and their introduction was probably due to literary and musical influences. The spelling *Leanore* or *Leanora* is also found. A short form which they share is **Nora**.

Leontine *see* Leo

Leopold *m.*

From the Old German words meaning 'people' and 'bold'. This name came to Britain through Queen Victoria's uncle, King Leopold of Belgium, after whom she named her fourth son. It has not been used much in the 20th century.

Leroy *m.*

A surname which comes from the Old French meaning 'the King' which was probably given to royal servants. It has been very popular as a first name in the United States, particularly amongst Black Americans in recent years.

Leslie, Lesley *m. and f.*

These were respectively the usual masculine and feminine spellings of the name, although they are both now used for girls. It is a Scottish surname, perhaps meaning 'garden of hollies', used originally by the Lords of Leslie in Aberdeenshire. It was taken into general use as a first name in the late 19th century.

Lester *m.*

This is a form of the town name Leicester used as a first name. The town is an ancient one, and its name indicates that it is a Roman town in the territory of the Ligore clan.

Letitia *f.*

From the Latin meaning 'gladness'. *Lettice* was the usual form of this name from the 12th to the 17th centuries, during which time it was very popular. In the 18th century the Latin *Laetitia* superseded it, which is now more frequently spelt Letitia. The phonetic form is *Leticia,* and *Laeta* is also found. None of these names is common at present, though Lettice did return briefly in the late 19th and early 20th century. The short forms *Lettie* and *Letty* are sometimes used independently.

241

Leverne *see* **Latasha**

Lewis, Louis *m.*

From Old German *Chlodowig*, meaning 'famous warrior', which was latinized into Ludovicus, from which *Ludovic* derives. The Old French form, *Clovis*, was the name of the founder of the French monarchy. His name later became Louis, and this was the name of eighteen French kings. The Normans brought the name to England where it became Lewis. The use in this country of the French form, Louis, is comparatively recent, with Robert Louis Stevenson an early example; this form is quite common in the Scottish lowlands Short forms are *Lou* and *Louie*, or *Lew* and *Lewie*.

Lex *see* **Alexander**

Lia *see* **Leah**

Liam *see* **William**

Lianne, Leanne *f.*

A pet form of the name **Juliana**, via the French Julianne, which has become popular as an independent name. It can also be spelt *Liane* and occurs in such forms as *Leigh Ann*.

Libby, Liese, Liesel *see* **Elizabeth**

Lilian, Lily *f.*

Originally these names may have been pet forms of **Elizabeth**. *Lillian* is found in Shakespeare's time but the name was probably associated with the lily flower even then. In the 19th century Lily was definitely given as the name of the flower, which is a Christian symbol of purity. *Lil* is the usual abbreviation. Other forms of the name include *Lillah* or *Lila*, and, in Scotland, *Lillias*.

Lilith *f.*

From the Hebrew meaning either 'serpent' or 'belonging to the night'. In mythology, Lilith was an evil spirit who haunted the night and who had been Adam's rejected wife before Eve. The name has been used very rarely.

Lillah, Lillian, Lillias, Lily *see* **Lilian**

Lina *f.*

A short form of names ending in '-lina', such as Angelina and Carolina, used as an independent name.

Lin *see* **Linda, Lyn**

Linda *f.*

This was a common ending for girls' names in Old German, and comes from the word for a snake, an animal which was held in great reverence by primitive German tribes. It represented wisdom and suppleness, and the names derived from it were therefore complimentary. In Spanish *linda* means pretty, and this may also have had some effect on the use of Linda as an English first name, which only dates from the 19th century. It is also used as a contraction of **Belinda**. Linda is also spelt *Lynda*, while *Lindy*, *Lindi(e)*, *Lin* and **Lyn** are pet forms.

Lindsey *m. and f.*

From the Scottish surname meaning 'pool island'. Together with its other forms, *Lindsay*, *Linsey* and *Linsay*, this name is used for both boys and girls. The form Lindsay tends to be the more usual one for boys. At the moment all forms of the name are used more frequently for girls than for boys and can then take the form *Linzi*.

Lindy *see* Linda

Linet, Linete, Linnet *see* Lynette

Linn, Linne *see* **Lyn**

Linsay, Linsey, Linzi *see* **Lindsey**

Lionel *m.*

This name means 'young lion'. It is a French diminutive of *Leon* and thus derives from the same root as *Leo* . It was the name of one of King Arthur's knights and was given by Edward III to his third son, later Duke of **Clarence**. The name was very popular in the Middle Ages and survived into more recent times, particularly in the north of England, where it has come back into general, though infrequent, use.

Lisa, Lisette, Liz, Liza, Lizzy *see* **Elizabeth**

Llewellyn *m.*

This name derives from Welsh. The original form was *Llywelyn* and its meaning is doubtful but the form Llewellyn suggests that users thought it was connected with the Welsh word for 'lion'. It is an old Welsh name which was anglicized into *Leolin(e)* as early as the 13th century. This form was used at least until the 17th century. **Lyn** is a short form.

Lloyd *m.*

A Welsh name meaning 'grey'. *Floyd* is a variant form which has arisen due to the difficulty of pronouncing the Welsh 'll', and which appears to come from the USA.

Llywelyn *see* Llewellyn

Lo *see* Dolores

Lochie, Lochlann *see* Lachlan

Lois *f.*

In the New Testament Lois was the grandmother of **Timothy**. As the rest of the family had Greek names, Lois is probably Greek also, but its meaning is not known. Like many obscure biblical names, it was taken into use in the 17th century by Puritans. It fell out of use but was revived at the beginning of the 20th century.

Lola *f.*

This was originally a diminutive of the Spanish **Dolores** and of Carlotta (see **Charlotte**). The pet form, *Lolita*, has become well known in the 20th century through Vladimir Nabokov's novel of that name.

Lolita *see* **Dolores, Lola**

Lolly, Lora, Lorel, Loretta *see* **Laura**

Loraine *see* **Lorraine**

Lorcan *see* **Laurence**

Loren *see* **Laura, Laurence**

Lori *see* **Laura, Lorraine**

Lorna *f.*

This name was created by R.D. Blackmore for the heroine of his novel, *Lorna Doone*, published in 1869. He may have had in mind both the Marquis of Lorne and the old English word meaning 'lost, forsaken'. The name of the actor, *Lorne* Green showed the masculine version.

Lorraine *f.*

This is the French district, whose name derives from the Old German place name Lotharingen, meaning 'Lothar's place'. Lothar was an Old German warrior name meaning 'famous army'. Lorraine is the form used in France. In Britain and North America it sometimes takes the forms *Loraine*, *Laraine* or *Lauraine*. *Lori* is a pet form.

Lottie, Lotty *see* **Charlotte**

Lou, Louie *see* **Lewis, Louisa**

Louella *see* **Luella**

Louis *see* **Lewis**

Louisa, Louise *f.*
Louise is the French, and Louisa the Latin female form of Louis (see **Lewis**). Though common much earlier in France, Louise did not come to Britain until the 17th century when Louise de Keroual became Charles II's mistress. It was popular for about a century until Louisa replaced it. Today Louise is popular, particularly as a second name. Pet forms are *Lulu*, *Lou* and *Louie* (see also **Luella**).

Lucas *see* **Luke**

Lucasta, Lucette, Lucia *see* **Lucy**

Lucia *see* **Lucy**

Lucille *f.*, **Lucius** *m.*
From the Latin word *lux*, meaning 'light' (see **Lucy**). *Lucilla* retains the Latin form, while Lucille

is French. The male form Lucius and its variants, *Lucien* and *Lucian*, are much less common than the feminine names.

Lucina *see* **Lucy**

Lucinda *f.*
Originally a poetic form of **Lucy**, this name is now given independently, and has recently become quite popular. The short forms **Cindy**, *Cindi* or *Cindie* are sometimes used as names in their own right.

Lucretia *f.*
This is a Roman family name. Its use as a first name in Renaissance Europe was due to the story of the Roman matron, Lucretia, who was raped by Tarquin and committed suicide as a result. This incident led to the expulsion of the ruling Tarquin family from Rome and the foundation of the Roman republic. Shakespeare's poem, *The Rape of Lucrece*, spread the use of the name in this form. It was common in Britain between the 16th and the 18th centuries but has never quite died out.

Lucy *f.*
Lucy is the usual English form of the Latin *Lucia*

from *lux*, meaning 'light'. In Roman times the name often signified that the child had been born at dawn; the goddess *Lucina* was the patroness of childbirth, bringing the children into the light of day. St Lucy was a Sicilian martyr who was much beloved in the Middle Ages, and the name became well established after the Norman Conquest. Diminutives are *Lucette*, **Lucinda**, *Lucasta* and *Lulu*.

Ludovic *see* Lewis

Luella *f.*
A blend of the names **Louise** and **Ella**. Today the name is most popular in North America. *Louella* is an alternative spelling.

Luke *m.*
A Greek name, latinized as *Lucas*, meaning 'a man of Lucania' in southern Italy. St Luke the Evangelist is the patron saint of doctors and also of painters, and the name was often given by a craftsman to his son. The name appeared in the 12th century as Lucas but a century later it was well established in the English form, Luke.

Lulu *see* Louisa, Lucy

Luned *see* **Eluned, Lynette**

Luther *m.*
From the Old German, meaning 'people's warrior'. The modern use of Luther as a first name is entirely due to Martin Luther, the great German religious leader of the Reformation, and to the American civil rights campaigner Martin Luther King, named after him.

Lydia *m.*
From the Greek meaning 'a Lydian girl'. Lydia was a district of Asia Minor where the people were famous merchants, and were said to have invented coinage. In the Acts of the Apostles, Lydia was a widow of Philippi who was converted by St Paul when he stayed at her house. The name was not used in this country before the 17th century.

Lyn *f. and m.*
A short form of such names as **Linda**, **Lynette** and **Carolyn** when used for girls. It can also take the form *Lin*, *Linne*, *Linn*, *Lynn* and *Lynne*. As a boy's name it can take the form Lyn or Lynn and is derived either from a surname or from a short form of **Llewellyn**.

251

Lynda *see* **Linda**

Lynette *f.*

From the Welsh name **Eluned** via its short form, Luned. The form Lynette was introduced by the poet Tennyson in the story of 'Gareth and Lynette' in his *Idylls of the King*. It is also spelt *Linet*, *Linnet*, *Linette* and *Lynnette*, and **Lyn** is used as a short form.

Lynn, Lynne *see* **Lyn**

Lynnette *see* **Lynette**

M

Mabel *f.*

Mabel is a shortening of **Amabel**, with *Mabella* as the Latin form. Both were current from the 12th to the 15th century, but were rare thereafter until Mabel was revived in the 19th century and became very common. It then suffered another fall from favour. The pet form often used is **May**. *Maybelle* and *Maybelline* are developments of the name.

Macsen *see* **Maximilian**

Madel(e)ine *f.*

Magdalene, the original form of the name, is Hebrew and means 'woman of Magdala', a town on the Sea of Galilee which was the birthplace of St Mary Magdalene. From about the 12th century the name was used in England in the French form Madeline, often abbreviated to Maudlin and

Madlin. *Magdalen*, the biblical form, was adopted after the Reformation. It was usually pronounced Maudlin, but because the meaning of this word developed the sense of 'weak and sentimental', this form was replaced by the current pronunciation. It shares the short form *Madge* with **Margaret**. *Maddie* or *Maddy* is also used. A Continental short form is *Magda*, which has also been given as an independent name.

Madge *see* Madeline, Margaret

Madoc, Madog *m.*
A Welsh name meaning 'fortunate'. It is rarely used outside Wales (see also **Marmaduke**).

Madonna *see* Donna

Mae *see* May

Mael Moire *see* Miles

Maeve *f.*
The more usual phonetic form of the Irish name *Meadhbh*, meaning 'she who makes drunk'. It was the name of a famous queen in Irish legend. A diminutive is *Meaveen*, and the name is occasionally spelt *Meave* or *Mave*.

Magda, Magdalen(e) *see* **Madeline**

Maggie *see* **Margaret**

Magnus *m.*
This is a Latin adjective meaning 'great'. The
spread of this name was due to the Emperor
Charlemagne, *Carolus Magnus* in Latin. Some of
his admirers took Magnus for a personal name,
and among those who christened their sons after
him was St Olaf of Norway. The name spread from
Scandinavia to Shetland and Ireland. From
Shetland the name became well established in
Scotland. In Ireland it became *Manus*, hence the
common Irish surname McManus.

Mahalia *f.*
A form of the Hebrew *Mahala* meaning
'tenderness'. No longer a very unusual name, it is
best known from the singer, Mahalia Jackson.

Mai *see* **May**

Maia *see* **Maya**

Mair, Maire *see* **Mary, Moira**

Mairead *see* **Margaret**

Mairi *see* **Mary**

Mairin *see* **Maureen**

Maisie *see* **Margaret**

Maja *see* **Maya**

Malcolm *m.*
From the Gaelic *mael Colum*, meaning 'follower of
St Columba'. This was a very popular Scottish
name, and four kings of Scotland bore it. It was
used very occasionally in medieval England, but it
was only in this century that it became common.
Short forms are *Mal* and *Col(u)m* (see **Calum**).

Malvina *f.*
A name invented by the Scottish poet, James
Macpherson (1736-96). He may have meant it to
be understood as from the Gaelic meaning
'smooth brow'. The form *Melvina* is also found.

Mamie *see* **Mary**

Mandy *see* **Amanda**

Manny *see* **Emanuel**

Manon *see* **Mary**

Manuel *see* **Emanuel**

Manus *see* **Magnus**

Maol Mhuire *see* **Miles**

Marc, Marcel *see* **Marcus**

Marcia *f.*

The feminine form of the Latin *Marcius*, a Roman clan name which probably was derived from Mars, the god of war. St Marcia was an early Christian martyr. The name can either be pronounced with three syllables, or with two, reflected in the alternative spelling *Marsha*. *Marcy* is used as a short form. *Marcella*, *Marcelle*, *Marcelline* and *Marcine* are all developments of the name.

Marcus, Mark *m.*

These names are probably derived from Mars, the Roman god of war, and were used as Roman family and personal names. Although it occurs from the Middle Ages in Britain, Mark has only become common since the 1950s. The Latin form, Marcus, is the less common of the two, but has recently had a certain popularity with parents. The

French forms *Marc* and *Marcel*, the latter derived from the Latin diminutive of the name, Marcellus, are also used in Britain today.

Marcy *see* Marcia

Maredudd *see* Meredith

Margaret *f.*

From the Latin *margarita*, derived from the Greek word meaning 'a pearl'.However, the ultimate origin is said to be Persian for 'child of light'; the ancients believing that pearls were formed when oysters rose from their beds at night to look at the moon, and trapped a drop of dew in their shells which was then transformed into a pearl by the moonbeams. The name first appears in Scotland in the 11th century, thanks to St Margaret, wife of Malcolm III. She was born in Hungary where the name had spread through respect for St Margaret of Antioch, a 3rd-century martyr. The name became very common in medieval England and, after a decline, regained popularity in the 19th century. The most common pet forms are *Maggie*, *Madge*, *Meg* and *Peg(gy)*. *Maisie* was a particularly Scottish variant, and *Megan* Welsh. The Irish form is *Mairead* ('mar-ed'). Other diminutives sometimes used are the Swedish **Greta**, French *Margot* (now also spelt *Margaux*) and *Marguerite*, and **Rita**, from *Margarita*, which is also the source of the Scandinavian pet form *Meta*. Other forms include *Marghanita*, *Margaretta* and *Margoletta* (see also **Daisy**, **Margery**, **May**, **Pearl**).

Margery, Marjorie *f.*
Margerie was originally a pet form of the French Marguerite (see **Margaret**), but it became established as a proper name in England as early as the 12th century. Marjorie is the spelling in Scotland, where the name was popular from the late 13th century after Robert Bruce gave the name to his daughter. She later founded the **Stuart** dynasty by marrying Walter the Steward. *Marge* and *Margie* are pet forms.

Marghanita, Margot, Margoletta *see* Margaret

Marguerite *see* Margaret, Margery

Mari, Maria *see* Mary

Mariam, Mariamne *see* Miriam

Marian *f.*

Marian or *Marion* was originally a diminutive of the French, Marie (see **Mary**), which was early established as an independent name, and was common on both sides of the Channel in medieval times. Marian was later extended to *Marianne*, giving rise to the double name *Mary Anne* in the 18th century. *Marianna* is the Spanish equivalent, which is sometimes given in England. In the USA *Marion* is occasionally found as a boy's name, as in the case of Marion Morrison, the real name of actor John Wayne (1907-79). In such cases it is using the surname Marion as a first name, possibly influenced by Francis Marion who played an important part in the American War of Independence.

Marie, Mariel, Mariella, Marielle, Marietta, Mariette *see* Mary

Marigold *f.*

This name, borrowed from the flower, was adopted with others in the late 19th century, but has never been common.

Marilyn *f.*

This name is a diminutive of **Mary** that is now

used independently. Its popularity was heightened by the film actress, Marilyn Monroe (1926-62).

Marina *f.*

From the Latin *marinus*, meaning 'of the sea'. The name has been used occasionally from at least the 14th century, probably on account of St Marina of Alexandria, a martyr of the Greek church. The name became more popular in Britain in 1934, when Prince George married Princess Marina of Greece, who later became Duchess of Kent.

Mario *see* Marius

Marion *see* Marian

Marisa, Marise, Marissa *see* Mary

Marius *m.*

From a Roman family name which was adopted as a first name during the Renaissance. It has never been common in this country, although *Mario* is very popular in Italy. The name is probably derived from Mars, the Roman god of war.

Marjorie *see* Margery

Mark *see* Marcus

Marlene *f.*

is a German shortening of Mary Magdalene (see **Madeleine**). It was introduced to English speakers by the song *Lili Marlene* and by the actress Marlene Dietrich (1901-1992). *Marlena* is a form which reflects the German pronunciation of the name, but a two syllable pronunciation, the second half of the name sounded as in the word 'lean' as opposed to the German 'lane', is common in this country (see also **Arlene**).

Marlon *m. and. f.*

A name of unknown origin, brought into use through the fame of the actor, Marlon Brando (b. 1924). *Marlin* and *Marlo* have also been used for both sexes in the United States.

Marmaduke *m.*

From the Irish *mael Maedoc*, meaning 'servant of **Madoc**'. The name is mainly confined to Yorkshire, where Celtic civilization lingered after the Norse invasions of the north of England. *Duke* is sometimes used as an abbreviation, but in America its use is usually derived from the title.

Marsha *see* Marcia

Martha *f.*

From the Aramaic, meaning 'lady'. In the New Testament Martha was the sister of Lazarus and Mary Magdalene. The name was common in France in the Middle Ages where there was a legend that Martha had come to France after the Crucifixion. It was not adopted in Britain until after the Reformation. Variants include *Marta* and *Martella*. *Martie* is the commonest pet form.

Martin *m.*, Martina *f.*

From the Latin *Martinus*, a diminutive of *Martius* meaning 'of Mars', the Roman god of war. According to popular legend, St Martin was a 4th-century soldier who cut his cloak in half to share it with a beggar one winter's night. Martin later became Bishop of Tours in France. Martin has been used more or less without a break since the 12th century. *Martyn* is the Welsh spelling, and *Marty* a short form. *Martina* and *Martita* are the female forms of the name. *Martinella* and the French feminine *Martine* are also found for girls.

Marvin *see* Mervyn

Mary *f.*

A biblical name, traditionally meaning 'dew of the

sea', but possibly going back to an ancient Egyptian name. The earliest form of the name was Miriam which later translations of the Bible changed to Mariam and Maria, and finally Mary. The name was held to be too sacred for general use until about the 12th century when the French form, Marie, and the diminutive, **Marian**, were common. The Scots kept the French *Marie* and used the Gaelic *Mairi* and *Mhairi* or *Mhari*. *Maire* is the Irish form, and *Mair* or *Mari* the Welsh. The latinized *Maria* was adopted in the 18th century, giving a pet form of *Ria*. *Marise* and *Maris(s)a* are Continental forms of the name. Other elaborations are *Mariel(le)*, *Marietta*, *Mariette*, and *Mariella*. Pet forms of Mary are *Molly*, *Polly*, *Mimi*, *Mamie* and **May**, with *Manon* a French pet form (see also **Marian**, **Marilyn**, **Maureen**, **Maya**, **Mia**, **Miriam**, **Moira**). While Mary is still popular as a second name, it is little used as a first name today. A recent trend has been to adopt the Continental habit of linking Marie with another name, to produce names such as Marie-Rose and Marie-Louise.

Maryann, Maryanne, Mary Anne *see* Marian

Matilda *f.*

From the Old German meaning 'mighty in battle'. This name was particularly popular in medieval Court circles, introduced by William the Conqueror's wife who bore the name. Later, their granddaughter, sometimes known as **Maud**, fought her cousin Stephen for the throne. The name fell into disuse but returned to favour in the 18th century. *Matty* and *Tilly* are pet forms. Although by no means common, there has been a recent increase in the the use of this name.

Matthew *m.*

From the Hebrew meaning 'gift of God', and the name of one of the Evangelists. The name was particularly popular from the 12th to the 14th centuries. After the Reformation the Greek form, *Matthias*, was adopted. In the Bible it is used for the name of the apostle chosen to succeed Judas Iscariot. Today the English form is popular, and the usual short form is *Matt*.

Matty *see* Matilda

Maud *f.*

The Old French form of the name **Matilda**. This name was popular in Britain after the Norman

Conquest, but fell out of use about the 15th century. It was revived in the 19th century by Tennyson's well-known poem, *Maud* (1855). It is also spelt *Maude*, and *Maudie* is sometimes used as a pet form.

Maura *see* Moira

Maureen *f.*

A phonetic form the Irish *Mairin*, meaning 'little Mary'. The variant forms in Britain are *Moreen* and **Moira**. The Irish also have a name *Mor* meaning 'tall' which has a pet form *Moirin*, which can be anglicised as Moreen.

Maurice, Morris *m.*

From the Latin *Mauritius*, meaning 'a Moor'. The spread of the name was due to St Maurice, a 3rd-century martyr in Switzerland, after whom the town of St Moritz was named. The Normans brought the name to England as Meurisse, which was soon anglicized to Morris. The more modern French form, Maurice, has now to a large extent replaced the English form, although it is usually pronounced the same way.. There is a Welsh equivalent, *Meurig*, which occurs from the 5th century. Short forms are *Morrie* and *Maurie*.

Mave see **Maeve**

Mavis f.
This comes from the old word for a song thrush. It was first used by Marie Corelli in her novel *The Sorrows of Satan* (1895), for a character called Mavis Clare (see also **Thelma**).

Max see **Maximilian, Maxwell**

Maximilian m.
Maximus in Latin means 'greatest'. Two 3rd-century saints bore the name Maximilian derived from it, but despite this, it is popularly thought to have been invented by the German Emperor Frederick III, combining the last names of Quintus Fabius Maximus, and Scipio Aemilianus, two great Roman generals. His son, later Emperor Maximilian I, was a reckless huntsman and fighter, and his name became very popular in German-speaking countries. The name has recently become more popular in this country, particularly in its short form, *Max. Macsen* is the Welsh form of Maximus. *Maxime* is used in France for both sexes, but in Britain this, or *Maxine*, tends to be used for girls, keeping *Maxim*, also a Russian form of the name, for boys.

Maxwell *m.*

From a Scottish surname, which derives from a place name meaning 'Mac's well'. It has been given as a first name since the end of the last century. *Max* is the short form.

May *f.*

This was originally a pet form of **Mabel**, **Margaret** or **Mary** but it has more recently been associated with the month (see **June**), and it is now a separate name. Variants are *Mae*, as in the actress Mae West (1892-1980), and *Mai* (see also **Avril**).

Maya *f.*

This is a respelling, reflecting the pronunciation, of the Scandinavian name *Maja*, a pet form of **Mary**. It is also found spelt *Maia*.

Maybelle, Maybelline *see* Mabel

Meadhbh, Meave, Meaveen *see* Maeve

Meg, Megan *see* Margaret

Mel *see* Melvin

Melanie *f.*

From the Greek meaning 'black' or 'dark-skinned'.

Melania is an ancient name used by both the Greeks and the Romans. This name came to England from France in the mid-17th century in its French form, Melanie, which also became *Melony* or *Mel(l)oney* and *Melany* in Britain.

Melicent, Melisenda, Melisande, Melisent see Millicent

Melissa *f.*

From the Greek meaning 'a bee' and the name of a nymph in Greek mythology. It was used occasionally in the 18th century, and has been quite popular in recent years. Other names with the sense of 'bee' or 'honey' that are used are *Melinda* and *Melita*.

Melloney, Meloney, Melony see Melanie

Melody *f.*

This vocabulary word has come into use as a first name in recent years.

Melvin, Melvyn *m.*

Various theories have been put forward as the the source of this name. It seems likely that it comes from a surname, which can come from a variety of sources, several of them Scottish. *Mel* is the short form.

Melvina *see* Malvina

Mercedes *see* Dolores

Mercy *f.*
This is the virtue used as a first name, in the same way as **Hope**. The pet form is *Merry*, which is also used as an independent name. The old-fashioned *Mercia* can either be a form of this or be from the Anglo-Saxon kingdom of Mercia, which covered the Midlands.

Meredith *m. and. f.*
From the surname from the ancient Welsh name *Maredudd* or *Meredydd*, meaning 'great chief'. It is sometimes spelt *Meridith*, and shares *Merry* with **Mercy** as a short form. Use of the name for girls is a 20th-century innovation.

Meriel *see* Muriel

Merle *f.*
This is the French for 'blackbird' originally derived from Latin. It was adopted as a first name in the 19th century. It became well known as the name

of the film actress, Merle Oberon (1911-79). In the USA it is used sometimes as a boy's name.

Merlene, Merlin, Merlyn *see* **Mervyn**

Merrill *see* **Muriel**

Merry *see* **Mercy, Meredith**

Mervyn *m.*
From the Welsh name *Myrddin* ('sea fort'), which is the true form of *Merlin*, the name of King Arthur's legendary magician. It is also spelt *Mervin*. Merlin has recently come to be used for girls, sometimes in the forms *Merlene* or *Merlyn*. *Marvin*, also a common surname, is probably a form of Mervyn, although some would dispute this.

Meryl *see* **Muriel**

Meta *see* **Margaret**

Meurig *see* **Maurice**

Mhairi, Mhari *see* **Mary**

Mia *f.*
A Scandinavian pet form of **Mary**, although some

associate it with the Italian and Spanish word for 'my'. The actress, Mia Farrow, brought the name into more general use.

Michael *m.* Michelle *f.*

From the Hebrew meaning 'who is like the Lord?'. In the Bible Michael was one of the seven archangels and their leader in battle, and he therefore became the patron of soldiers. The variant form *Micah*, the name of a minor prophet in the Old Testament, was used in the 17th century among Puritans. Michael has pet forms *Mike*, *Mick*, *Micky*. The surname *Mitchell*, derived from Michael, is also used as a boy's name, with the short form, *Mitch*. Michelle is the French female form of the name, also found as *Michele*, which can be shortened to **Shelley**. *Michaela* is another feminine form of the name. *Misha* or *Mischa* is in Russia a pet form of Michael, but because of the 'a' ending is sometimes thought of as a girl's name here.

Mildred *f.*

The 7th-century King Merowald of the Old English kingdom of Mercia had three daughters: Milburga ('gentle defence'), Mildgyth ('gentle gift'), and Mildthryth ('gentle strength'). It was from the last of these that Mildred was derived and the popularity of the three sisters, all of whom became saints, led to the name becoming common in the Middle Ages. It was revived in the 19th century.

Miles *m.*

An old name of unknown meaning. The Normans brought to Britain the forms Miles and *Milo*. It has also been used to transliterate the Irish *Maol Mhuire* ('devotee of Mary') and its Gaelic form *Mael Moire*. A variant spelling is *Myles*.

Milla *see* Camilla

Millicent, *f.*

From the Old German meaning 'strong worker'. This name was common in France about a thousand years ago, when it had the form *Melisenda*, now also *Melisande*. The French brought it to England in the late 12th century in the form *Melisent*, and it survived with minor changes of spelling such as *Melicent* well into the 17th century. In the 19th it was revived. *Millie* or *Milly* is a common abbreviation.

Millie, Milly *see* Amelia, Camilla, Emily, Millicent

Milo *see* Miles

Milton *m.*

From the Old English surname, itself derived from a place name meaning 'mill-enclosure'. Its use as a first name may initially have been due to the fame of the poet, John Milton (1608-74). It has been particularly popular in America.

Mima *see* Jemima

Mimi *see* Mary

Minna, Minnie *see* William

Minta, Minty *see* Araminta

Mira *see* Myra

Mirabel, Mirabelle *f.*

From the Latin meaning 'admirable, wonderful'. The Latin form *Mirabella* was used in the last century, but it was later anglicized to Mirabel.

Miranda *f.*

From the Latin meaning 'deserving admiration'. This name was coined by Shakespeare for the heroine of *The Tempest* (1612), a young girl blessed with many admirable qualities. Like other Shakespearian names it has come into use in the 20th century.

Miriam *f.*
This is the old form of **Mary**, and in the book of Exodus in the Old Testament it was the name of the sister of **Moses** and **Aaron**. It is traditionally interpreted as meaning 'dew of the sea', but possibly, like Miriam's brothers' names, goes back to ancient Egyptian sources. It first became common in Britain in the 17th century. *Mariam* and *Mariamne* are variant forms which have recently gained popularity. *Mitzi* can be a short form of Miriam or Maria.

Mischa, Misha, Mitch, Mitchell *see* Michael

Mitzi *see* Miriam

Moira, Moyra *f.*
Moira or *Maura* is an English phonetic spelling of *Maire*, the Irish form of **Mary**. **Maureen** has the same origin, but has developed as a separate name, though Moira is occasionally used as a short form of Maureen.

Moirin *see* Maureen

Molly *see* Mary

Mona *f.*
This name is derived from a diminutive of the Irish *Muadhnait* ('mooa-nid'), meaning 'noble, good'. It came into use in the late 19th century along with other Irish names which spread throughout Britain at that time, during a general revival of interest in Celtic culture. It can also be a short form of **Monica**.

Monica *f.*
The etymology of this name is uncertain, but it could be connected with Greek *monos* meaning 'alone' or Latin *monere* meaning 'to advise'. St Monica was the mother of St Augustine and was a paragon of motherly virtues. **Mona** is sometimes used as a short form, and there are French and Scandinavian forms, *Monique* and *Monika*.

Montagu(e) *m.*
The founder of this ancient and noble family was Drogo de Montacute, a companion of William the Conqueror, who was granted estates in Somerset. He took his name from Mont Aigu, a 'pointed hill' in Normandy. The use of Montagu(e) as a first name dates from the 19th century, when many

aristocratic surnames were adopted by the general public, e.g. **Cecil**, **Howard**, **Dudley**, **Mortimer**, **Percy**. It shares *Monty* as a short form with **Montgomery**.

Montgomery *m.*
From the Old French, meaning 'mountain of the powerful one'. While mainly a surname, it has occasionally been used as a first name in the last hundred years. *Monty* is a short form.

Montserrat *see* Dolores

Monty *see* Montague, Montogmery

Mor *see* Maureen, Morag

Morag *f.*
A Scottish name, from the Gaelic and Irish name *Mor* meaning 'great, tall'.

Moray *see* Murray

Morcant *see* Morgan

Moreen *see* Maureen

Morgan *m. and. f.*
In its earliest form, *Morcant*, this name meant

277

'sea-bright' (see **Muriel**), but it later absorbed another name, *Morien*, meaning 'sea-born'. Its earliest celebrated male bearer was the first recorded British heretic, who was known as Pelagius, a Greek translation of the name. It was almost always a male name until this century, but now seems to have become part of the modern trend to use traditional boys' names for girls. The most famous female precedent for the name was Morgan(a) le Fay, King Arthur's wicked half-sister.

Morna, Myrna *f.*
Both these names come from the Gaelic name *Muirne*, which means either 'gentle', the traditional interpretation, or possibly 'high spirited'.

Morrie, Morris *see* **Maurice**

Mortimer *m.*
An aristocratic surname adopted as a first name in the 19th century. The surname was derived from a French place name meaning 'dead sea'. The Mortimer family connect it with the Dead Sea in Palestine, where their ancestors fought in crusading times. The pet form, *Morty*, was also used independently in Ireland as a form of the

Irish name *Murtaugh* or *Murty* ('skilled sailor').
The short form *Mort* is also used.

Morven *f.*
A Scottish name, from an old name for the
northwest of the country. In legend, it is the name
of **Fingal**'s kingdom. It means 'high mountains'.

Morwenna *f.*
From Welsh and probably means 'maiden'. There
was a 5th-century saint of this name about whom
little is known, and the name used to be confined
to Wales and Cornwall, but now seems to be
spreading. It is also found as *Morwen*.

Moses *m.*
The meaning of this name is uncertain and it is
possibly Egyptian rather than Hebrew. It became
common among Jews after their return from
captivity in Babylon. In Britain it first appears in
the Domesday Book as Moyses, which became
Moyse or *Moss* in general use. The present form,
Moses, which was not used until the Reformation,
is the form used in the Authorized Version of the
Bible.

Moyra *see* **Moira**

Muadhnait *see* **Mona**

Muirne *see* **Morna**

Mungo *m.*

This name was originally a term of affection given
to St **Kentigern** by his followers, and in Gaelic
means 'beloved'. Kentigern was a 6th-century
bishop of Glasgow and is generally known as St
Mungo. The name is confined to Scotland and the
most famous bearer was Mungo Park, the 18th-
century explorer of the River Niger.

Murdo, Murdoch *m.*

This Scottish name is derived from the Gaelic
meaning 'seaman', and is equivalent to the Irish
Murtaugh (see **Mortimer**).

Muriel, Meriel *f.*

A Celtic name meaning 'sea-bright'. The name
came to England at the time of the Norman
Conquest, via the many Celts who had settled in
Brittany and Normandy in earlier centuries. Both
forms were in common use until the mid-14th
century. Muriel was revived in the 19th century

and Meriel came back into use at the beginning of this century. Other forms such as *Meryl* and *Merrill* have appeared more recently.

Murray *m.*

From the Gaelic meaning 'sea'. The Scottish clan of Murray, or Moray, probably took its name from the Moray Firth in the northeast of Scotland. James Stuart, Earl of Moray, was half-brother of Mary Queen of Scots, and he acted as Regent when she was imprisoned in Loch Leven Castle. His fame gave rise to the use of *Moray* as a first name in Scotland, but today the form Murray is more common, with *Murry* a variant.

Murtaugh, Murty *see* Mortimer

Myfanwy *f.*

A well-known Welsh name meaning 'my fine one'. The commonest short forms in Wales are *Fanny* and *Myfi*.

Myles *see* Miles

Myra *f.*

This name appears to have been invented in the 16th century by Fulke Greville, Lord Brooke, for the heroine of his love poems, and until the 19th

century it was used exclusively by poets and
novelists. He may have wanted to echo the sound
of 'admired'. The variant form, *Mira*, is found but
this can also be a short form of **Mirabel** or
Miranda.

Myrddin *see* **Mervyn**

Myrna *see* **Morna**

Myrtill, Myrtilla *see* **Myrtle**

Myron *m.*
The Greek word for 'fragrant'. It was the name of
a famous sculptor in the 5th century BC.

Myrtle *f.*
One of the flower names which has been used as
a name since the 19th century. The name is
Greek, and in Ancient Greece the myrtle was a
symbol of victory, while in the last century, myrtle
was a traditional element in a bride's bouquet.
The variant form *Myrtill(a)* is also found
occasionally

N

Nadine *f.*
A French name, derived from the Russian for 'hope'. It is occasionally found in Britain, but only in this century. Variant forms are *Nada* and *Nadia*.

Nan *see* Anne

Nancy *f.*
This was originally a pet form of **Anne**, but has long been established as a name in its own right. *Nancie* is occasionally found, and *Nanette* and *Nana* are French forms.

Nandy *see* Ferdinand

Nanette, Nanny *see* Anne, Nancy

Naomi *f.*
From the Hebrew meaning 'pleasant'. In the Old Testament Naomi was the mother-in-law of Ruth,

and loved her daughter-in-law so much that when
their menfolk died, she left her home to travel
back to Israel with Ruth. The name was adopted
by the Puritans in the 17th century and has
recently increased in popularity.

Nat *see* **Nathan, Nathaniel**

Natalie, Natalia *f.*
These names come from the Latin *natale domini*,
meaning 'the birthday of the Lord', and were
originally restricted to children born around
Christmas. The name comes from Russia where it
is spelt *Natalya*, and has the pet form *Natasha*,
currently the more popular form of the name in
this country. This is sometimes spelt *Natacha* or
Natasja, and can have the short form *Tasha*.
Natalia can be shortened to *Talia*, *Talya* or *Tally*.

Nathan *m.*
From the Hebrew meaning 'gift'. It was the name
of the prophet in the Old Testament who
condemned King David for putting Uriah in the
front line of battle to get him killed, so David could
marry his widow, Bathsheba. It has recently
become more popular. The name shares the short
form *Nat* with **Nathaniel**.

Nathaniel *m.*

From the Hebrew meaning 'gift of God'. It was the name of the apostle who was better known by his second name, **Bartholomew**. It was rare in Britain until after Shakespeare's use of it in *Love's Labour Lost* (1594) but it is more common in North America today than in Britain. *Nat*, the short form, is shared with **Nathan**.

Neal, Neil *see* Nigel

Ned, Neddy *see* Edward

Neirin *see* Aneurin

Nell, Nelly *f.*

These are pet forms of **Helen** and **Eleanor**. They were already in use in Britain in the Middle Ages. A famous holder of the name was Nell (Eleanor) Gwyn, the mistress of Charles II.

Nelson *m.*

A surname meaning 'Neil's son' (see **Nigel**). It is used as a first name in memory of Horatio Nelson (1758-1805).

Nerissa *f.*

This is one of the less common names taken from

Shakespeare, in this case **Portia**'s witty maid from *The Merchant of Venice*. It is not clear what Shakespeare meant by the name, but he may have taken it from *nereis*, the Greek word for a sea-nymph.

Nerys *f.*
An unusual Welsh name, meaning 'lady', which has become widely known through the actress, Nerys Hughes.

Nessa, Nessie, Nest, Nesta *see* Agnes

Net *see* Anthony, Janet

Netta *see* Janet

Nettie *see* Anthony, Janet

Neville *m.*
From the French surname Neuville, meaning 'new town'. It was introduced into England at the time of the Norman Conquest, when the Neville family, which came over with William the Conqueror, was very powerful. Their influence continued, but the name was not adopted as a first name until the 17th century. *Nevil* is a variant spelling.

Niall *see* Nigel

Niamh *f.*
This name, pronounced 'nee-av' or 'neev', is currently a very popular name in Ireland. It means 'radiance, brightness' and was originally the name of a pagan goddess. In Irish legend Niamh was a fairy woman who fell in love with **Ossian** and carried him off to the magical Land of Promise.

Nichola, Nichole *see* Nicola

Nicholas *m.*
From the Greek meaning 'victory of the people'. The name was common in the Middle Ages as a result of the popularity of St Nicholas, the patron saint of children and sailors. The usual form then was *Nicol.* In Latin the name is Nicholaus and the use of *Claus* in 'Santa Claus' is taken from *Klaus,* the modern German development of the Latin. *Nick* and *Nicky* are the pet forms. (See also **Colin**, **Nicola**).

Nicola, Nicole *f.*
These are the Italian and French female forms of **Nicholas**. The names are also spelt *Nichola* and *Nichole,* and *Nicolette* is also used. *Nickie*, *Nikki*

and *Nicci* are short forms shared with Nicholas (see also **Colette**).

Nigel, Niall, Neal, Neil m.

The origin of these names goes back to an Irish name, the meaning of which could be 'champion', 'cloud' or 'passionate'. Niall is the Irish spelling of the name, but it early on developed different spellings. When medieval scribes wanted to write the name in Latin documents they gave it the form *Nigellus*, as if it were a name which came from the Latin *niger* meaning 'black'; and when interest was strong in all things medieval in the 19th century, this Latin form was adopted as Nigel. Nigel has rare girl's forms, *Nigella* and *Nigelia*.

Nikki, Nicci, Nickie see Nicola

Nina f.

A pet form of various Russian names ending '-nina', which is now established in this country as a name in its own right.

Ninian m.

The name of a 5th-century saint who converted the Picts in the south of Scotland to Christianity. It is mainly found in Scotland.

Nita *see* **Joanna**

Noah *m.*
Despite the wide fame of Noah and his Ark, this Hebrew name meaning 'rest' is quite rare, perhaps because the events of Noah's life after the flood made the name seem less attractive to parents.

Noel *m. and. f.*
This is an old French name derived from the Latin *dies natalis*, meaning 'birthday'. The name refers to Christmas Day and was often given to children born then. *Nowell* is an English spelling which is also used and *Noelle* is an alternative girl's form. *Christmas* is also found occasionally as a first name.

Nola *see* **Fenella**

Nona *see* **Anne**

Nora(h) *f.*
An Irish abbreviation of **Honoria**, now used as a separate name. It is also found as a short form for **Eleanor** and **Leonora**. In Ireland the pet forms *Noreen* and *Nonie* are used.

Norm *see* **Norman**

Norma *f.*
Possibly from the Latin meaning 'rule' or 'precept'.
The great success of Bellini's opera *Norma* (1831)
brought the name into popular favour. It has been
used as a feminine counterpart of **Norman**.

Norman *m.*
From the Old English for 'Northman', used first of
all for the Vikings, and then for the descendants of
the Viking settlers in France who were known as
'Normans'. It was popular in Scotland, and for a
while was considered a purely Scottish name,
being used as a substitute for the Gaelic *Tormod*
('protected by Thor'), itself originally a Viking
name. *Norm* and *Norrie* are short forms.

Nowell *see* **Noel**

Nuala *see* **Fenella**

Nye *see* **Aneurin**

O

Oberon *see* **Aubrey**

Octavia *f.* **Octavius** *m.*
A Roman family name derived from the Latin
meaning 'eighth'. It was also used as a given
name for an eighth child in the 19th century, but
now that such large families are rare it is used
without regard to its original sense. *Octavian* is an
alternative masculine form.

Odette, Odile *see* **Ottilie**

Odysseus *see* **Ulysses**

Oengus *see* **Angus**

Oisin *see* **Ossian**

Ol, Ollie *see* **Oliver**

Olaf *see* **Oliver**

Olga *f.*

From the Norse word *helga*, meaning 'holy'. The founder of the Russian monarchy is supposed to have been a Scandinavian traveller, and it was in Russia that Olga evolved from the Scandinavian form, **Helga**. St Olga was the wife of the Duke of Kiev in the 10th century, and she helped spread Christianity in Russia.

Oliva, Olive *see* Olivia

Oliver *m.*

In Old French legend Oliver was the name of one of Charlemagne's greatest knights. Since these knights were of Frankish origin – that is to say of Germanic ancestry – their names are likely to be from Old German. Thus it is thought that this name goes back to the same source as the Scandinavian, *Olaf* ('heir of his ancestors'). However, users probably associate it with the more obvious source of the olive tree, symbol of peace. Oliver was popular until the parliamentary revolution led by Oliver Cromwell in the 17th century, after which the name fell out of favour. It was revived in the 19th century and is now very popular. *Ol* and *Ollie* are short forms. *Havelock* is said to be the Welsh form of the name.

Olivia *f.*

The female form of **Oliver**, but even more strongly associated with the Latin *oliva*, meaning 'olive'. St *Oliva* was venerated as the protectress of the olive crops in Italy. Olivia was first found in England in the early 13th century, was used by Shakespeare in *Twelfth Night*, and is currently very popular. *Olive* is a rarer form, although well-known as the name of the cartoon character, Olive Oyl, Popeye's girlfriend.

Olwen, Olwyn *f.*

From the Welsh, meaning 'white foot-print'. The name first occurs in an old Welsh legend in which Olwen, a giant's daughter, is wooed by a prince, who has to get help from King Arthur to do the tasks that are set him. She was named Olwen because white clover sprang up wherever she trod. The name became very popular in Wales and spread to England in 1849 when a new translation of the story was published.

Oona, Oonagh *see* Una

Ophelia *f.*

From the Greek meaning 'help'. Its use is due to Shakespeare's *Hamlet* (1601). In the play, Ophelia

293

is the girl who loves Hamlet but who goes mad after he murders her father and abandons her, and is finally drowned.

Oriel, Oriole *see* Aurelia

Orla *f.*
An Irish name meaning 'golden princess'. It also occurs as *Orlagh* and in the Old Irish spelling, *Orlaith*, and is currently very popular in Ireland.

Orlando *m.*
This is the Italian form of **Roland**. Italian names were fashionable in the 16th century and Shakespeare used this one in his play *As You Like It* (1600). It has become rather more common recently.

Orson *m.*
From the Old French *Ourson*, meaning 'little bear'. This is not a common name, though it is familiar through Orson Welles (1915-85), the American actor and director.

Orville *m.*
This is a name invented by the 18th-century novelist, Fanny Burney, for the hero of her novel *Evelina*. It is a fairly rare name in Britain. A famous

American example was Orville Wright, the
aviation pioneer and brother of **Wilbur**.

Osbert *m.*
From the Old English, meaning 'bright god'. It
shares *Oz* and *Ozzy* as pet forms with **Oswald**.

Oscar *m.*
In the 1760s James Macpherson gave the name to
Ossian's warrior son in his poems on the
legendary past of Scotland, and Napoleon's
enthusiasm for the Ossianic legend caused him to
give the name Oscar to his godson, later King of
Sweden. It became widespread on the Continent,
and was regularly used in England and Ireland.
The trial of Oscar Wilde in 1895 for homosexuality
caused an abrupt fall in the name's popularity in
Britain, but it remained in use in the United States,
and it is coming back into use here. The name
probably means 'deer-lover'.

Ossian *m.*
In legend Ossian ('little deer') is the son of **Finn**
and father of **Oscar**. It is spelt *Oisin* in Irish, while
Osheen reflects the Irish pronunciation, although
it is usually pronounced as it is spelt in England. A
female form *Ossia* also exists.

Oswald *m.*

From the Old English meaning 'god power'. Oswald, King of Northumbria in the 7th century, was killed fighting the Welsh at Oswestry. He was later canonized, and the place is said to take its name from him. A second St Oswald helped St Dunstan with his church reforms in the 10th century. Because of these two saints, the name was popular in the Middle Ages and has never entirely died out. *Oz* and *Ozzy* are used as pet forms shared with **Osbert**.

Ottilie *f.*

This is a modern form of *Ottilia*, which comes from the Old German meaning 'prosperity'. St Ottilie is the patron saint of Alsace. *Ottoline* is another form of the name, and the French *Odette* and *Odile* have also been used in Britain. The Continental male form, *Otto*, is less common in this country.

Owen, Owain *m.*

This is one of the most popular of all Welsh names, but its origin is uncertain. It may well have come from the Greek name **Eugene** meaning 'well-born', or from Welsh *oen*, meaning 'lamb'. There are many bearers of the name in Welsh history and legend, but the best known is Owen Glendower, who fought for Welsh independence in the 15th century. The name has spread to the rest of Britain and to North America.

Oz, Ozzy *see* Osbert, Oswald

P

Paddy *see* **Patrick.**

Paloma *f.*
This means 'dove', the symbol of peace. Its use by the artist, Pablo Picasso, for his daughter made the name more widely known.

Pamela *f.*
From the Greek meaning 'all honey'. This name only dates from the late 16th century when it was coined by Sir Philip Sydney for his romance *Arcadia*. It did not come into general use until the publication of Samuel Richardson's novel *Pamela* (1740). It has been most used in the 20th century, and *Pam* is the usual pet form.

Pandora *f.*
In Greek legend Pandora ('all-giving') is a beautiful but foolish woman created by the gods

to plague mankind. She opened the box that contained all the ills that afflict mankind. After their escape, only hope, which had been sealed up with them, was left to help mankind.

Pansy *f.*
The flower name used as a first name. It comes from the French *pensée*, meaning 'a thought'.

Pascal *m.*, **Pascale** *f.*
A French name meaning 'Easter', which has come into general use in this country since the 1960s.

Pat *see* **Patricia**, **Patrick**

Patience *f.*
This name was fashionable in the 17th century when girls were named after abstract virtues and Sir Thomas Carew could call his four daughters Patience, Temperance, Silence and Prudence.

Patricia *f.*
The feminine of Latin *patricius*, meaning 'nobleman'. It was originally only used in Latin records to distinguish a female bearer of the name **Patrick** then used for both sexes, but it was used independently from the 18th century. It has become common only in the last hundred years,

possibly encouraged by the popularity of Queen Victoria's granddaughter Princess Patricia of Connaught. Current abbreviations are *Pat*, *Patsy*, *Patti(e)*, *Patty* and *Tricia*.

Patrick *m.*

From the Latin *patricius*, meaning 'nobleman'. St Patrick adopted this name at his ordination. He was born in the late 4th century, captured by pirates when still a boy and sold as a slave in Ireland. Although he escaped, he wished to convert the Irish to Christianity, so after training as a missionary in France, he returned to devote his life to this cause. *Pat* and *Paddy* are short forms.

Patsy, Patti, Pattie, Patty *see* Patricia

Paul *m.*

From the Latin *paulus*, meaning 'small'. The New Testament tells how **Saul** of Tarsus adopted this name after his conversion to Christianity. The name was not common until the 17th century. It was often coupled with the name Peter, as the saints Peter and Paul share the same feast day. Today the name is quite popular as a second name, but few parents choose it as a first name.

Paula, Paulina, Pauline *f.*

These are the female forms of **Paul**. There was a
4th-century St Paula who founded several
convents in Bethlehem, and thus established the
name in the Middle Ages. Paulina and Pauline or
Paulette are respectively the Latin and French
forms. *Polly* is sometimes used as a pet form.

Pearl *f.*

This name first became common in the 19th
century, with other gem names such as **Beryl** and
Ruby. It has also been used as a pet name for
Margaret, which is derived from the Greek for
'pearl'. In America it has occasionally been used
as a man's name.

Peg, Peggy *see* Margaret

Penelope *f.*

In Greek legend Penelope was the name of
Odysseus's faithful and astute wife, who waited
ten years for her husband to return from the
Trojan Wars. The name has been used regularly
since the 16th century. It is often abbreviated to
Pen or *Penny*.

Perce *see* Perceval, Percy

Perceval, Percival *m.*

The name Percival first occurs in the Old French Arthurian romances of Chrétien de Troyes in the 12th century, where it is the name of a successful seeker of the Holy Grail. Chrétien interprets the name as *perce-val*, 'one who pierces the valley'. However, when used as a surname, Perceval probably refers to Percheval, a place in Normandy. The name has been used in this country since the 14th century. The short forms are *Perce* or **Percy**, and sometimes *Val*.

Percy *m.*

This famous northern family is descended from William de Perci, one of William the Conqueror's companions who took his name from a village in Normandy. Initially its use as a first name was confined to those connected with the Percy family, but during the 19th century it came into general use, partly due to the poet, Percy Bysshe Shelley. It shares the short form, *Perce*, with **Perceval** and is also a short form of this name.

Perdita *f.*

This is from the Latin meaning 'lost'. It was coined by Shakespeare for the heroine of *A Winter's Tale*, who was lost at birth.

Peregrine *m*.

From the Latin *peregrinus*, meaning 'stranger' or 'traveller' and hence 'pilgrim'. There was a 7th-century saint of this name who was a hermit near Modena in Italy. The name has been used in this country since about the 13th century, but it has always been rather uncommon. **Perry** is used as a short form.

Persephone *see* Corinna

Perry *m*.

This name sometimes occurs as an abbreviation of **Peregrine**, but it is also a surname used as a first name. It was the surname of two 19th-century American admirals, one of whom inflicted a defeat on the British while the other led the expedition that opened up Japan to the west. Their exploits probably encouraged the use of the name in the US. The singer, Perry Como, who helped spread the popularity of the name, was born Pierino, a pet form of **Peter**.

Peter *m*.

From the Greek *petras*, meaning 'rock'. Cephas is the Aramaic equivalent which Jesus gave as a nickname to Simon bar Jonah, to symbolize steadfastness in faith. Peter was chief of the Apostles and became the first Bishop of Rome. He was a favourite saint of the medieval church and his name was very popular throughout Christendom. In England the name is first recorded in the Domesday Book in the Latin form, *Petrus*. The Normans brought over the French form, **Piers** which was usual until the 14th century, when Peter became predominant, although Piers is now quite fashionable once again. The name was unpopular after the Reformation because of its association with the Papacy and did not return to fashion until 1904, when James Barrie's *Peter Pan* was published. A short form is **Pete**. *Peta*, *Petra* and *Petrina* are modern female forms of the name.

Petronella, Petronilla *f.*

These are derived from Petronius, a Roman family name. Petronilla, a 1st-century martyr, came to be connected with St **Peter**, and was even thought by some to be his daughter; because of this, the name was popular in the Middle Ages and used as the female equivalent of Peter.

Petula *f.*

Possibly from the Latin term meaning 'seeker'. It

is a very rare name but the singer, Petula Clark, made the name well known.

Phebe *see* Phoebe

Phelim *see* Felix

Philip *m.*
From the Greek meaning 'lover of horses'. It was common in the Middle Ages on account of the Apostle of that name. In Elizabeth I's reign Philip of Spain was the arch enemy of England, and the name suffered accordingly. It was revived in the 19th century. *Phil* is now the most usual short form, although *Pip* and *Flip* are sometimes used. *Phillip* is a variant spelling which reflects the form usually found in surnames.

Philippa *f.*
This is the female form of **Philip**, but originally was only used to distinguish women (who shared the name Philip with boys in the Middle Ages) in Latin records. Its use as a separate name dates from about the 19th century n and is now quite popular. Often abbreviated to *Pippa*, an Italian form, it can be found as *Phillippa* and *Philipa*. *Philippine* is a much rarer female form of Philip.

Phillip *see* **Philip**

Phillippa *see* **Philippa**

Phillis *see* **Phyllis**

Philomena *f.*
This name comes from the Greek for 'beloved'. It used to be a popular name in Ireland, but is now rather out of fashion. It was thought that there were two saints of this name, but when it was realised that the word Philomena on the inscription on their graves was an address to the reader and not their names the cult was suppressed; hence the name's fall from favour.

Phoebe *f.*
From the Greek meaning 'the shining one'. It is one of the titles given to the Roman moon goddess, **Diana**. It occurs as a personal name in St Paul's Epistle to the Romans and, perhaps for this reason, was adopted after the Reformation, reaching its peak of popularity in the 17th century. It is currently enjoying another rise in popularity and sometimes spelt phonetically **Phebe**. It can be used as a pet form of **Euphemia**.

Phyllis, Phillis *f.*
From the Greek meaning 'leafy'. In legend it was the name of a girl who died for love and was transformed into an almond tree. *Phyllida* is an alternative form which is sometimes found.

Pia *f.*
From the Latin meaning 'pious'. It was not used by English speakers until well into this century.

Piers *see* **Peter**

Pip *see* **Philip**

Pippa *see* **Philippa**

Polly *see* **Pauline, Mary**

Poppy *f.*
The flower used as a name. It was particularly popular at the end of the 19th century and the beginning of the 20th, and is once again becoming fashionable.

Portia *f.*
Portia is an old Roman family name with the unfortunate meaning of 'pig'. However, Portia, wife of Brutus, became famous for her stoicism

and bravery, which probably inspired Shakespeare to choose this name for the heroine of *The Merchant of Venice*. This Portia is beautiful, rich, wise, witty and charming, and it is thanks to her that the name has come into use as a modern girl's name.

Primrose *f.*

This flower name was popular at the beginning of the 20th century. *Primula* is a rare variant.

Priscilla *f.*

This is the Latin diminutive of *prisca*, which means 'ancient'. It was the name of a woman mentioned in the Acts of the Apostles and as with other New Testament names it was a favourite with the 17th-century Puritans. It also appears as *Prisca* but this form is very rare. *Pris* and *Prissy* are sometimes found as short forms, but *Cilla* is the most used variant.

Prudence *f.*

Prudence first appears as a name in Chaucer's books, and it was one of the first abstract virtues to be adopted by the Puritans. It is usually abbreviated to *Prue* or *Pru*.

Prunella *f.*
Probably from the Latin *prunus*, meaning 'little plum'. It is also the name of a kind of silk and the Latin name for a wild flower, the self-heal, and a bird, the hedge sparrow or dunnock. The actress, Prunella Scales, has made the name more widely known. It shares short forms with **Prudence**.

Q

Queenie f.

This name is sometimes given independently, but it is really a pet name for **Regina**, which is Latin for 'queen'. Regina was used from the Middle Ages, possibly with reference to the Virgin Mary, Queen of Heaven. Queenie was also used as a nickname for girls christened **Victoria** during Queen Victoria's long reign.

Quentin, Quintin m.

From the Latin for 'fifth', originally to have been given as a name to a fifth son. Quentin was the French form which the Normans introduced to England. It became obsolete after the Middle Ages except in Scotland, although it revived in the 19th century, possibly due to Sir Walter Scott's historical romance *Quentin Durward* (1823). *Quinton* is another form of the name.

Quincy *m.*
A surname taken from a French placename. Its use in the United States may have been due to the prominent New England family of that name in colonial times. John Quincy Adams (1767-1848), the country's sixth President, may have received his middle name in honour of this family or it may have been taken from Quincy, Massachusetts where he was born. It can also be found as *Quincey*.

R

Rab, Rabbie *see* **Robert**

Rachel *f.*
From the Hebrew for 'ewe', which was a symbol of gentleness and innocence. In the Book of Genesis, Rachel was 'beautiful and well-favoured', and Jacob laboured seven years to win her (Gen. XXIX. 20). In Britain the name was adopted after the Reformation and it was very popular in the 17th and 19th centuries. The usual pet forms today are *Rach*, *Rachie*, *Rae*, *Rai* and *Ray*, and it can be spelt *Rachael*. The actress, *Raquel* Welch, shows the Spanish form of the name. From Rachel have developed the forms *Rachelle* (sometimes pronounced with a 'sh' sound) and *Rochelle*, the French for 'little rock', a place name taken from Brittany to the USA where the name is popular. **Shelley** is a short form.

Rae, Rai *see* **Rachel, Raymond**

Raelene *see* **Darlene**

Ralph *m.*

From the Old Norse words meaning 'counsel' and
'wolf'. In its earlier form, Radulf, this name was
fairly common in England before the Norman
Conquest, and it was reinforced by French use.
The medieval spellings were *Ralf* and *Rauf* which
were pronounced with the same vowel sound as
the word 'ray'. *Rafe* was the common form in the
17th century and Ralph appears in the 18th
century. The current usual pronunciation with a
short 'a' and pronouncing the 'l' is 20th-century
practice. *Raoul* is the French form of the name.

Ramona *see* **Raymond**

Ranald *see* **Ronald**

Randolph *m.*

From the Old English Randwulf, meaning 'shield
wolf', which in the Middle Ages became *Ranulf*
and *Randal(l)*. The short form, *Randy*, has been
used as a name in its own right, particularly in the
USA.

Raoul *see* **Ralph**

Raquel *see* **Rachel**

Rastus *see* **Erasmus**

Rauf *see* **Ralph**

Ray *see* **Rachel, Raymond**

Raymond *m.*

From the Old German meaning 'counsel
protection'. The Normans brought the name to
Britain and it was particularly popular in
crusading times. Two 13th-century saints bore the
name. One of them spent much of his life rescuing
Spaniards captured by the Moors. **Redmond** or
Redmund is a form of the name which developed
in Ireland. The short form, **Ray**, is sometimes
given independently. There is a feminine form
Raymonde which also has the short forms **Ray**,
Rai and **Rae**. The Spanish female form is
Ramona.

Rebecca *f.*

In the Old Testament **Rebekah** (the Hebrew form
of the name) was the wife of **Isaac** and was
famous for her beauty. It was a favourite name
among Puritans, who took it to North America. It

is occasionally spelt **Rebekka** and is currently a very popular name. **Becky** is the short form.

Redmond, Redmund *see* Raymond

Reg, Reggie *see* Reginald

Regina *see* Gina, Queenie

Reginald *m.*
From the Old English *Regenweald*, meaning 'power force'. This was not a common Anglo-Saxon name, but it was reinforced at the time of the Norman Conquest by the French equivalent **Reinald** or **Reynaud**, and developed into **Reynold**. This was quite common up to the 15th century, by which time Reginald was replacing it. This appears first as Reginaldus, a Latin form of Reynold and a more formal alternative to it. Neither name was common between the 15th and 19th centuries, but Reginald was then revived and became very common. It can be abbreviated to **Reg**, **Reggie** or **Rex**.

René, Renée *m. and f.*
These are French boy's and girl's names derived from the Latin *renatus*, meaning 'reborn'. The Latin form was sometimes used by Puritans in the

17th century, and the French forms have been used in Britain in the 20th century. The Latin feminine form, *Renata*, is also used occasionally.

Renie *see* Irene

Reuben *m.*
From the Hebrew meaning 'behold a son', and it appears in the Bible as the name of a son of Jacob, the founder of one of the tribes of Israel. The form *Ruben* is also found.

Rex *m.*
This is the Latin for 'king' which has only been used as a first name in recent times. It is also found as an abbreviation of **Reginald**.

Reynard *m.*
From the Old German, meaning 'mighty and brave'. This and Rainard were the Norman French forms, but they never became as common as Reynold (see **Reginald**), with which they were often confused. It is very rare today, except as a term for a fox, due to one of the characters in Aesop's fables with this name.

Reynaud, Reynold *see* Reginald

Rhiannon *f.*
The name of an important figure in medieval
Welsh literature. There is evidence that she was
originally a Celtic goddess connected with horses.
The name means 'great queen, goddess' and is
spreading outside Wales. The old form was
Riannon, and the new form, *Rhianna*, is also
found.

Rhoda *f.*
Derived from the Greek for 'rose', this is a New
Testament name (see Acts X. 11-13) that was
taken into use in the 17th century. It was popular
in the early years of this century.

Rhodri *see* **Roderick**

Rhona *see* **Rowena**

Rhonda *f.*
This is a simplified spelling of the Welsh placename, Rhondda, which has been used as a first
name since the early part of this century.

Rhonwen *see* **Rowena**

Rhydderch *see* **Roderick**

Rhys

An old Welsh name meaning 'rashness, ardour'. It is a name with many famous bearers, including a Prince Rhys who checked the Norman advance into Wales.

Ria *see* **Mary**

Rian *see* **Ryan**

Riannon *see* **Rhiannon**

Richard m.

This name first appears in Anglo-Saxon as Ricehard meaning 'strong ruler', which was later developed into Ricard. It was the Normans who spread the present form of the name, the softer, French Richard. The short form, *Dick*, appears as early as the 13th century, and this is still very common, though *Rich(ie)*, *Dickie*, *Rick(ie)* and *Dickon* have been used at various times. Female forms of the name include *Richelle*, *Richenda* and *Ricarda*.

Rick, Rickie, Ricky *see* **Derek, Eric, Richard**

Riona *see* **Catriona**

Rita *f.*

This is an abbreviation of Margarita (see **Margaret**). However, it is used much more often as a separate name, and some of its popularity in the present century may have been due to its use by the film star, Rita Hayworth (1918-87).

Robert *m.*

This name is derived from the Old German meaning 'famous and bright'. Although there was an equivalent Anglo-Saxon name, it was the French form which took hold in Britain after the Norman Conquest. Robert the Bruce popularized the name in Scotland where it has the local short forms *Rab* and *Rabbie*. *Rob*, *Robbie*, *Bob*, **Bobbie** or *Bobby* and **Bert** are used in England. *Robin* or *Robyn*, a French diminutive of Robert which came to Britain in the Middle Ages, is now equally popular in its own right and used for both sexes, the 'y' form being most common for girls (see also **Rupert**).

Roberta, Robina *f.*

These are female forms of **Robert** and Robin. Both have been popular, particularly in Scotland. **Bobbie** and *Robin* or *Robyn* have become popular names derived from them.

Robin, Robyn *see* **Robert, Roberta**

Rochelle *see* **Rachel**

Rod, Roddy *see* **Roderick, Rodney**

Roderick *m.*

From the Old German meaning 'famous rule'. The Goths took the name to Spain where it became Rodrigo, and it was established there at least as early as the 8th century. In Britain the name is most common in Scotland where it was originally used to transliterate a Gaelic name, *Ruairi*. In Wales it is used as *Rhodri*, meaning 'crowned ruler' or *Rhydderch* ('reddish-brown'). Short forms are *Rod*, *Roddy* and **Rory**.

Rodge *see* Roger

Rodney *m.*

This means 'reed island', and was originally a surname. It was not used as a first name until Admiral George Rodney gave it heroic associations in the 18th century. Short forms are *Rod* and *Roddy*.

Roger *m.*

Hrothgar, meaning 'famous spear', was an Anglo-

Saxon form of this name, famous as the name of a legendary king, but it was the Normans who gave us the present form, which was derived from Old German. Roger was a favourite name in the Middle Ages, but from the 16th to the 19th centuries it was thought of as a peasant name. The ancient short form, *Hodge*, once a type-name for a farm labourer, has been replaced by *Ro(d)ge*.

Roisin *see* Rose

Roland, Rowland *m.*

From the Old German *Hrodland*, meaning 'famous land'. Roland was the most famous of Charlemagne's warriors, and the Normans brought the name to England. *Rowland*, currently a popular variant, is both the medieval spelling and the form of the surname which comes from this name. They are shortened to *Roly* or *Rowley*. **Orlando** is the Italian version of the name.

Rolf *m.*

From the Old German meaning 'famous wolf'. *Rollo* is a Latin form and Rollo the Ganger ('Walker') was a 9th-century Norwegian exile who, with his followers, founded the Norman race. Rolf developed in Normandy and came to Britain at the time of the Norman Conquest. It was quite quickly absorbed into **Ralph**, but was revived in the late 19th century.

Roly *see* Roland

Romey, Romy *see* Rosemary

Rona *see* Rowena

Ronald *m.*
Ronald and *Ranald* are Scottish equivalents of Reynald and **Reginald**, but they are from the Norse (Viking) not the Old English forms. Ranald is still almost exclusively Scottish but Ronald is now widespread. Short forms commonly used are *Ron* and *Ronnie*.

Rory, Rorie *m.*
From the Irish and Gaelic *Ruairi*, meaning 'red-haired'. The name became popular in Ireland due to the fame of the 12th-century King Rory O'Connor. It is also widely used in the Scottish Highlands, and is sometimes used in England as an abbreviation of **Roderick**. It can also be spelt *Ruari* and *Ruari(dh)*

Rosa, Rosabel, Rosabella, Rosalba *see* Rose

Rosalie *f.*

From Latin *rosalia*, the name of a Roman festival when garlands of roses were draped on tombs. Its use as a first name is due to St **Rosalia**, a 12th-century hermit, the patron saint of Palermo in Sicily. Rosalie is the French form.

Rosalind *f.*

The origin of this name is the Old German *Roslindis*, either made from elements meaning 'horse and serpent' or 'fame and shield' – the experts disagree. When the Goths took it to Spain it was interpreted as *rosa* and *linda*, 'pretty rose', and it was with this meaning that it came over to Britain in Elizabeth I's reign. It was used by Shakespeare for the heroine of *As You Like It* and in another form, **Rosaline**, in two other plays. Largely due to this literary association it has been popular ever since. It has developed a number of different forms such as **Rosalyn**, **Rosalin**, **Rosalinda**, **Roslyn** and **Rosaleen** which is used in Ireland as an alternative form of Roisin (see **Rose**). A short form is **Roz**.

Rosamund, Rosamond *f.*

This comes from the Old German words meaning 'horse' and 'protection', but it has generally been associated with the Latin *rosa munda*, meaning 'pure rose' or *rosa mundi*, 'rose of the world'. The Normans brought the name to England. A short form is *Roz*.

Rosanna(h), Rosanne *see* **Roseanne**

Rose *f.*

This flower, the symbol of the Virgin Mary, has been the most popular of all flower names which are used as personal names, but it has an older and quite different derivation. Its source is the Old German *hros*, meaning 'horse' (see **Rosalind**, **Rosamund**). The name was brought to England by the Normans, and it has been consistently popular, giving rise to many derivatives, like *Rosalba* ('white rose'), *Rosetta*, ('little rose'), and *Rosabel(la)* ('beautiful rose'), as well as *Rosina*, *Rosita* and the pet form *Rosie* or *Rosy*. *Rosa* is a Latin form which has been used occasionally since the 19th century. In Ireland *Roisin*, sometimes spelt *Rosheen* to reflect its pronunciation, and which means 'little rose', is popular. Rose is used as a short form of all the girl's names which begin with its sound. It is particularly common at the moment as a second name.

Roseanne *f.*

This is one of the many developments of **Rose**, here combined with **Anne**. Variants include *Roseanna*, *Rosanna*, *Rosanne* and *Rosannah*, as in Rose + **Hannah**.

Rosemary *f.*

This is generally considered to be a plant name, although it is sometimes analysed as a combination of **Rose** and **Mary**. The plant name is derived from the Latin *ros marinus*, meaning 'dew of the sea' which describes the misty blue-green of its leaves. It can be spelt *Rosemarie* and *Romy* or *Romey* and *Rosie* are short forms.

Rosetta, Rosheen, Rosina, Rosita *see* Rose

Rosie *see* Rose, Rosemary

Roslyn *see* Rosalind

Ross *m.*

From the Gaelic meaning 'of the peninsula', and the name of a famous Scottish clan. It has been most used in Scotland and Ireland, Canada and Australia.

Rosy *see* Rose

Rowan m. and. f.

From the Irish *Ruadhan*, meaning 'little red-(haired) one'. It was the name of an Irish saint. Once used exclusively for boys, it is now also found as a girl's name, in which case it can take the form *Rowanne*.

Rowena f.

Probably best thought of as a form of the Welsh *Rhonwen*, meaning 'fair (woman) slender as a lance'. Rowena was the daughter of the Saxon chief Hengist and her beauty bewitched the British king, Vortigern bringing about his downfall; she may have had a truly Saxon name, but her story is transmitted through Welsh-speaking British writers and seems to have taken on a Welsh form. Its modern use is due to Sir Walter Scott, who gave this name to the heroine of his novel *Ivanhoe* (1819). *Rowina* is another spelling. *Rhona* or *Rona* has been claimed as a short form of Rhonwen, although it is also the name of a Scottish island.

Rowland, Rowley *see* Roland

Roxana f.

This is the English form of a Persian name which

means 'dawn, light'. Roxana was the name of one of Alexander the Great's wives, and the marriage was said to be a love-match. *Roxane* and *Roxanne* are variants.

Roy *m.*
From the Gaelic *ruadh*, meaning 'red'. A well-known example of the name is the famous Highlander Robert Macgregor, commonly known as Rob Roy because of his red hair, who was involved in the Jacobite Rising of 1715. Sir Walter Scott's novel about him may have contributed to its popularity.

Roz *see* **Rosalind, Rosamund**

Ruadhan *see* **Rowan**

Ruairi, Ruari, Ruaridh *see* **Rory**

Ruben *see* **Reuben**

Ruby *f.*
This is one of many jewel names introduced during the 19th century.

Rudolf, Rudolph *m.*
From the Old German *Hrodulf*, meaning 'famous

wolf', the same name that gives us **Rolf**. Rudolf is the Modern German form of the name which has only been used in this country for about a hundred years. Earlier examples occurred only among German immigrants. The spread of this name was undoubtedly helped by the widespread adoration of Rudolf Valentino (1895-1926), the American film star. Another American, the singer *Rudy* Vallee (1901-86) made the pet form, found in Germany as *Rudi*, well known.

Rufus *m.*

This is a Latin word meaning 'red-haired'. William Rufus was the second son of William the Conqueror, and became King William II of England. It gained popularity as a given name during the 19th century.

Rupert *m.*

This name has the same origin as **Robert** and means 'bright fame'. In Germany, it became Rupprecht, and Rupert is an English form of this. Rupert of the Rhine was Charles I's nephew and a brilliant general. He came to England to support the Royalist cause and was much admired for his dashing bravery. It was because of him that the English form was coined and became popular.

Russell *m.*

This is primarily a surname and is derived from the Old French *rousel*, which means 'little red (haired) one'. It was a surname which came into use as a first name along with other family names in the 19th century. *Rus(s)* and *Rusty* are pet forms.

Ruth *f.*

A biblical name which came into common use just after the Reformation on account of the Old Testament heroine who gave her name to the *Book of Ruth*. The name is also associated with the abstract noun, ruth, meaning 'sorrow' or 'pity'. *Ruthie* is a pet form.

Ryan *m.*

A common Irish surname meaning 'little king', now used as a first name. Its spread was greatly helped by the success of the film star, Ryan O'Neal (b. 1941). It is also found as *Rian*.

S

Sabina *f.*
A Latin name meaning 'a Sabine woman'. It has been used in Ireland for the Irish *Sabhbh*, *Sive* in its phonetic spelling, meaning 'sweet'. There is also a French form, *Sabine*.

Sabrina *f.*
This is a very ancient name, used for the River Severn before the Romans came and probably the name of the goddess of the river. The poet, John Milton (1608-74), used it as the name of the nymph of the Severn in his masque *Comus*, and subsequent uses of it as a first name probably stem from this.

Sacha *m. and. f.*
Originally, a Russian short form of **Alexander**. Although originally a man's name, the 'a' ending has led to its use for girls. *Sasha* is an alternative form.

Sadie *see* Sarah

Saffron *f.*
The name of the golden-yellow crocus pollen used as a spice, which has come to be given as a first name in modern times.

Sally *f.*
Originally a pet name for **Sarah**, but one thatis nowadays used independently. It is shortened to *Sal*.

Salome *f.*
This is the Greek form of an Aramaic name meaning 'peace'. In the New Testament it is the name of one of the women at Jesus' tomb on Easter Sunday. However, the story of the Salome who danced the dance of the seven veils to persuade her step-father Herod to execute John the Baptist has given the name a bad reputation, and it is only rarely used.

Sam, Sammy *see* Samantha, Samuel

Samantha *f.*
Probably an 18th-century coinage, meant to be a feminine version of **Samuel**. It became popular in

the 1950s, when it appeared in the film *High Society* and in the title song, *I Love You, Samantha*.

Samuel *m.*

From the Hebrew meaning 'heard by God'. The Old Testament tells how the prophet was the leader of the Israelites and how he chose Saul and later David as their kings. In Scotland and Ireland it was for a long time used to transliterate the Gaelic *Somhairle*, anglicised as *Sorley*; this name derives from the Old Norse term meaning 'summer wanderer', that is, 'Viking'. It shares short forms *Sam* and *Sammy* with **Samantha**.

Sanchia *f.*

This is a Provençal and Spanish name derived from the Latin *sanctus*, meaning 'holy'. The name came to England in the 13th century when the Earl of Cornwall married Sanchia, daughter of the Count of Provence.

Sandra *f.*

This is a short form of Italian *Alessandra*, now used as a name in its own right (see **Alexandra**). *Sandie* or *Sandy* are pet forms. It also appears as *Sondra*, and the designer *Zandra* Rhodes uses an unusual alternative form.

Sandy *see* **Alexander, Sandra**

Sara(h) *f.*

Sarah comes from the Hebrew, meaning
'princess', and was the name of Abraham's wife in
the Old Testament. Sara is the Greek form found
in the New Testament. **Sally**, *Sal* and *Sadie* started
life as pet forms. In Ireland Sarah has been used to
render the Irish *Sorcha* ('sorr-ha', the 'h' as in
Scottish 'loch') meaning 'bright', and *Saraid*
('sahr-it') meaning 'excellent'.

Sasha *see* **Sacha**

Saskia *f.*

This was the name of the wife of the Dutch artist
Rembrandt (1606-69), whose paintings of her
introduced the name to this country. It may be
connected with the word for Saxon.

Saul *m.*

comes from the Hebrew meaning 'asked for
(child)'. The name occurs in the Old Testament as
that of the first King of Israel, and in the New
Testament as St **Paul**'s name before his
conversion to Christianity. It was initially used as a
first name in Britain in the 17th century.

Scarlett *f.*
The use of Scarlett as a first name is due entirely to the success of Margaret Mitchell's *Gone with the Wind*. In the novel, Scarlett O'Hara is given her grandmother's maiden name as a middle name, but always called by it. **Scarlet** is also used.

Scott *m.*
This is a surname, meaning 'a Scot', used as a first name.

Seamas *m.*
This is an Irish form of **James**. It is also spelt *Seamus* and the Gaelic form is *Seumas* or *Seumus*. *Shamus* is a modern phonetic version of the name (see also **Hamish**).

Sean *m.*
This is the Irish form of **John** and developed from the French Jean. It is also spelt as it is pronounced, *Shaun* or *Shawn*. *Shane* is a variant form.

Sebastian *m.*
From the Latin *Sebastianus*, meaning 'man of Sebasta'. The name of this town in Asia Minor was derived from the Greek meaning 'majestic' or 'venerable'. St Sebastian was executed by being

shot at with arrows, and his martyrdom was a
particularly popular subject for paintings. The
name took hold in Spain, and in France, where it
was shortened to *Bastien*, and taken across the
Channel from Brittany to the West Country by
fishermen. The form *Bastian* took root there. The
name did not spread to the rest of Britain until
modern times, but Sebastian is now reasonably
common, having the short forms *Seb* and *Sebbie*.

Selina *f.*

The etymology of this name is disputed. One
possible derivation is from *Selene*, the Greek
moon goddess; another is from the Latin name
Coelina from *caelum*, meaning 'heaven', through
the French form *Céline*. *Celina* is also found.

Selma *f.*

Selma is the name of a castle in James
MacPherson's 18th-century poems about Scottish
legendary heroes. When the poems were
translated into Swedish the translator failed to
make the meaning clear, and it was understood by
many Swedish readers to be a personal name, and
was subsequently used by some for their children.
Immigrants took the name to the United States,
where it is still more common than in Britain.

Seonaid see **Sheena**

Serena f.
This is a Latin word meaning 'calm, serene (woman)'.

Seth m.
This is a biblical name meaning 'appointed' which was given to the third son of Adam and Eve. It was popular with the Puritans who took it with them to America, where it shows some signs of returning to popularity.

Seumas, Seumus, Shamus see **Seamas**

Shane see **John, Sean**

Shani see **Sian**

Shannon f.
This is the Irish river and placename, meaning 'the old one', which has come to be used as a first name in recent years.

Sharlene see **Charlene**

Sharlott see **Charlotte**

Sharmaine *see* **Charmaine**

Sharon *f.*
In the Bible Sharon, which means 'the plain', is an
area of rich natural beauty and to compare a
woman to it came to be a great compliment. It has
been used as a first name only this century, but
has been very popular. It is occasionally spelt
Sharron.

Shaun, Shawn *see* **Sean**

Sheela *see* **Sheila**

Sheena *f.*
This is a phonetic form of **Sine**, the Gaelic for **Jane**.
An alternative form of Jane is **Siubhan**, which in
Irish becomes **Siobhan**, with phonetic spellings
Shevaun and **Chevonne**. **Shona**, the Scottish form
of **Janet**, comes from the same root and is a
phonetic form of **Seonaid**, in Irish **Sinead** (shin-
aid).

Sheila *f.*
A phonetic spelling of **Sile**, the Irish form of
Cecilia. It can also be spelt **Shelagh**, **Shiela** and
Sheela.

337

Shelley *f.*
is a pet form of **Michelle** and **Rachel** as well as
being a variant of the name **Shirley**. From the
1940s the name was brought to public attention
by the actress Shelley Winters.

Sheree, Sherrie, Sherry *see* **Cherie**

Sheril, Sheryl *see* **Cheryl**

Shevaun *see* **Sheena**

Shiela *see* **Sheila**

Shirley *f.*
This was originally a place name meaning 'shire
meadow'. From this it became a surname in
Yorkshire and elsewhere. It was primarily a boy's
name until Charlotte Bronte started the fashion for
it as a girl's name in 1849, when her novel *Shirley*
appeared (see also **Shelley**).

Shona *see* **Sheena**

Sian *f.*
is the Welsh form of **Jane**, properly spelt *Siân*.
Siani is a pet form which may appear as *Shani*.

Sibyl, Sibylla *see* Sybil

Sidney, Sydney *m. and. f.*

This is a surname used as a first name from at
least the beginning of the eighteenth century. The
spelling Sydney did not appear until the 19th
century, and the city in Australia was named after
Viscount Sydney, who was Secretary of State at
the time. The short form is *Sid*. In the 18th century
girls were given surnames as first names more
often than was usual until very recently, and
Sydney as a girl's name may date from this.
Alternatively, it may be a form of the Latin name
Sidonia('woman of Sidon'), which became *Sidonie*
in French and *Sidony* in English. In the US Sydney
is regarded primarily as a female name.

Silas *see* Silvester

Sile *see* Sheila

Silvester, Sylvester *m.*

Silvester is Latin for 'wood-dweller'. There have
been three popes of this name. The name was
quite common in both forms in the Middle Ages.
The New Testament name *Silas* is probably a form
of Silvester. Like so many names which were

popular with the Puritans, Silas is showing signs of coming back into fashion. *Sylvestra* and *Sylvana* are rare female forms.

Silvia, Sylvia *f.*

This is the Latin word meaning '(woman) of the wood'. Rhea Silvia was the mother of Romulus and Remus, the founders of Rome. This may have been the reason why the name was adopted during the Renaissance in Italy. Like other classical names, it came to England in Elizabethan times and Shakespeare used it in *Two Gentlemen of Verona*, and this probably gave rise to its use in Britain. The diminutive form is *Silvie* or *Sylvie*.

Simon *m.*, Simone *f.*

This is the better-known English form of the New Testament *Simeon*, the name of the man who blessed the baby Jesus in the Temple. The popularity of Simon in the Middle Ages was due to Simon **Peter**, the Apostle, whose popularity was great at that period. The short form is *Sim*. Simone is the feminine form taken from the French.

Sine, Sinead, Siobhan *see* Sheena

Sion *see* **John**

Sis, Sisley, Sissy *see* **Cecilia**

Siubhan *see* **Sheena**

Sive *see* **Sabina**

Somhairle *see* **Samuel**

Sondra *see* **Sandra**

Sonia *f.*
This is a Russian pet form of **Sophia**, and its use in Britain is modern, perhaps a result of the novel of this name by Stephen McKenna, published in 1917. *Sonya* and *Sonja* are other spellings of the name.

Sophia, Sophie *f.*
From the Greek meaning 'wisdom'. *Hagia Sophia* ('Holy Wisdom'), is a common dedication for Orthodox churches as in the case of the great cathedral at Constantinople. This led to Sophia's use as a name in Greece. The name spread through Hungary to Germany and then to England when George I became king. Both his mother and his wife had the name. Sophie is the anglicized

form which is currently the more popular. The form *Sophy* is also used (see **Sonia**).

Sorcha *see* Sarah

Sorley *see* Samuel

Stacey, Stacy *m. and. f.*
This is a pet form which has become popular as an independent name. For men it was a short form of **Eustace**; as a woman's name it was originally short for **Anastasia**.

Stanley *m.*
This was originally a surname derived from an old Anglo-Saxon place name meaning 'stony field'. It was used as a first name from the mid-19th century partly because of its association with Sir Henry Morton Stanley, the famous explorer. It has the short form *Stan*.

Stefan, Steffan *see* Stephen

Stella *f.*
This is the Latin word for 'star'. Its use is due to its literary associations. An early use was in Sir Philip Sidney's *Astrophel and Stella* (1591). Then, in the early 18th century, Jonathan Swift used it as a pet

name in letters to Esther Johnson. Other forms are
Estella and *Estelle*.

Stephen, Steven *m.*, Stephanie *f.*

From the Greek *stephanos* meaning 'crown' or
'wreath'. The laurel wreath was the highest
honour a man could attain in the classical world.
Stephen was a common personal name in Ancient
Greece, and it was borne by the very first Christian
martyr (Acts VI & VII). The name is first recorded
in this country in the Domesday Book and after
the Norman Conquest its popularity increased.
Steven is the alternative spelling, but at the
moment, more parents seem to be choosing the
'ph' form. *Steve* and *Stevie* are the modern pet
forms. There is also a Welsh form, *Steffan*, and the
Continental form, *Stefan*, is also used. The female
form, Stephanie, currently seems to be more
popular with parents than Stephen.

Stuart *m.*

From the Old English *sti weard*, an official who
looked after animals kept for food. Though it has
changed its meaning somewhat, it survives as
'steward' today. The man who founded the
Scottish royal house of Stuart in the 14th century
was William the Steward, who married the king's

daughter and whose son later became king. *Stewart* is a common alternative and *Stuert* is also used.

Susan, Susanna(h) *f.*
Shushannah is the Hebrew for 'lily' and Susanna(h) was the earliest form of this name in England, occurring in the Middle Ages and becoming quite common after the Reformation. Susan was adopted in the 18th century. In the 20th century the French forms, *Suzanne* and *Suzette*, have also been used in Britain, and spellings such as *Susana* and *Suzanna* have been found. *Sue*, *Sukey*, *Susie* and *Suzy* are pet forms.

Sybil *f.*
In classical times the Sibyls were prophetesses, and some of them were supposed to have foretold the coming of Christ. Because of this, *Sibylla* came to be used as a first name, the Normans bringing it with them to England. Sybil or *Sibyl* had a revival in the second half of the 19th century after Disraeli had published his political novel of that name (1845). The actress *Cybill* Shepherd has introduced another form of the name.

Sydney *see* Sidney

Sylvana, Sylvester, Sylvestra *see* **Silvester**

Sylvia, Sylvie *see* **Silvia**

Syril *see* **Cyril**

T

Tabitha *f.*
This name derives from the Aramaic word for
'gazelle'. In the New Testament (Acts IX) it is the
name of a Christian woman of Joppa who showed
great charity towards the poor, and was raised
from the dead by St Peter. The Greek form of her
name was **Dorcas**. *Tabatha* is a modern spelling
of the name.

Tadhg *see* **Timothy**

Taffy *see* **David**

Taliesin *see* **Ceridwen**

Talia *see* **Natalie**

Talitha *f.*
From an Aramaic word meaning 'girl'. It has very
occasionally been used in the 20th century.

Tally, Talya *see* **Natalie**

Tam *see* **Thomas**

Tamara *f.*
Tamara is the Russian form of the biblical name
Tamar, which means 'date palm'. Tamara was the
name of a famous Russian queen, and remains a
popular name in Russia. A pet form is **Tammy**.

Tammy *f.*
A pet form of **Tamara** and **Tamsin**, now used as
an independent name. In 1957 a film called
Tammy and a song of that name, which was the
bestselling record in the USA for three weeks,
started a vogue for the name's use. It is also a
Scottish form of Tommy (see **Thomas**).

Tamsin *f.*
This is a West Country female form of **Thomas**. It
can also be found as *Tamsine*, *Tamzin* and
Tamzen. It comes from *Thomasin* or *Thomasine*
which have been used since the Middle Ages.
Thomasina is an old latinized version which was
revived in the 19th century. **Tammy** is a short
form of these names.

Tania *see* **Tanya**

Tanith *f.*
The name of a Phoenician goddess of love that has recently come into occasional use as a first name. It can also take the form *Tanit*.

Tansy *f.*
The name of a yellow wild flower used as a first name. It can also be a pet form of **Anastasia**.

Tanya *f.*
Tanya or *Tania* is a pet form of *Tatiana*, which has been popular in Russia for many years. There were several saints named Tatianus, the masculine form, and a St Tatiana, a martyr revered by the Greek Orthodox Church. *Tonya* is also found although, properly, this is the Russian pet form of **Antonia**.

Tara *f.*
Tara is the name of the hill where the ancient High Kings of Ireland held court and which plays an important part in Irish legend. It has only been used as a first name since the end of the last century. Very occasionally, it has been used for boys.

Tasha *see* **Natalie**

Tatiana *see* **Tanya**

Ted, Teddy *see* **Edmund, Edward, Theodore**

Terence *m.*

This is from the Latin *Terentius*, the name of a famous Roman comic playwright. Short forms are *Terry* and *Tel*. It is now also found in the forms *Terance*, *Terrance*, *Terrence* and *Terrell* (although this could also be from the name of an American city). It is a comparatively modern name, having come from Ireland, where it was used to transliterate the native *Turlough* ('tar-loch', pronounced as if Scottish), meaning 'instigator' (see also **Theodoric**).

Teresa, Theresa *f.*

The meaning of this name is obscure. The first recorded Theresa was the wife of the 5th century St Paulinus, and was responsible for his conversion. The name was for a long time confined to Spain until the fame of St Teresa of Avila (1515-1582) spread the name to all Roman Catholic countries, but it did not become common in this country until the 18th century. It is often abbreviated to *Tess*, *Tessa* or *Tessie*. The form *Teri* or *Terry*, shared with some boys' names, is also found. A variant is **Tracy**. The French form, *Thérèse*, is also found occasionally.

Terrance, Terrell, Terrence *see* Terence

Terry *see* Terence, Teresa, Theodoric

Tess, Tessa, Tessie *see* Teresa

Thea *see* Dorothy, Theodora

Thelma *f.*
Like **Mavis**, this name was introduced in the 19th century by the writer Marie Corelli in her novel *Thelma* (1887), and spread quickly throughout the country. There is a Greek word *thelema* meaning 'will', which may have had some influence on its development.

Theo *m. and. f.*
This is a short form of *Theobald*, a Germanic name made up of elements meaning 'people' and 'bold', and of names such as **Theodore**; but it is increasingly being used as an independent name. If used for girls it comes from **Theodora**.

Theodora *f.*
This is the feminine form of **Theodore**, which has

been used since the 17th century. It is usually abbreviated to **Theo**, **Thea** and **Dora**. The rarer *Theodosia* has a similar meaning.

Theodore *m.*

From the Greek meaning 'gift of God'. There are 28 saints of this name in the Church Calendar. In England the name did not become general until the 19th century, but in Wales it has long been used as a form of *Tudur* or *Tudor*, which in fact probably comes from a Celtic name. The usual abbreviation in North America is *Ted* or *Teddy*, as in the case of President Theodore Roosevelt who gave his name to the teddy bear. In England **Theo** is a more common abbreviation.

Theodoric *m.*

From the Old German meaning 'people's ruler'. The Old English form of the name was Theodric which in medieval times became *Terry*, and in French *Thierry*. Theodoric became the most common form in the 18th century, but it is rare in Britain today (see also **Derek**, **Terence**).

Theodosia *see* **Theodora**

Theophania *see* **Tiffany**

Theresa, Thérèse *see* Teresa

Thierry *see* Theodoric

Thomas *m.*

From the Aramaic nickname meaning 'twin'. It was first given by Jesus to an Apostle named Judas to distinguish him from Judas Iscariot. In England it was originally used only as a priest's name until the Norman Conquest, after which it became common. The abbreviation *Tom* appears in the Middle Ages. *Tam* and **Tammy** are the Scottish pet forms. The use of *Tommy* as a nickname for a British private soldier goes back to the 19th century, when the enlistment form had on it the specimen signature 'Thomas Atkins'. Thomas has been one of the three top boy's names for some years.

Thomasin, Thomasina, Thomasine *see* Tamsin

Thora *f.*

From the Norse meaning 'Thor-battle'. Its earlier form was *Thyra*. In Norse mythology, Thor was the god of thunder in Norse mythology, and he also gave his name to 'Thursday'. Thora is a rare name in Britain, but well known from the actress, Thora Hird.

Thurstan *see* Dustin

Thyra *see* Thora

Tiffany *f.*
Originally a pet form of the name *Theophania*, from the Greek meaning 'the manifestation of God'. Tifainé was the Old French form, and this name was given to girls born at the time of the Epiphany, the words having the same meaning. These names were rare until recently when Tiffany became a popular name.

Tilly *see* Matilda

Timothy *m.*
Timotheos is an old Greek name meaning 'honouring God'. Its use as a first name is due to Timothy, the companion of St Paul. It was not used widely until the 16th century when many classical and biblical names were introduced. *Tim* and *Timmy* are the abbreviations. *Timothea* is a rare female form. In Ireland Timothy has for a long time been used as an equivalent for the native *Tadhg* ('tieg') which means 'poet'.

Tina *f.*
Originally a short form for girls' names ending in '-tina', commonest of which is Christina (see **Christine**). It is now used as a name in its own right.

Titus *m.*
This is a Latin name of unknown meaning. Two well-known holders of the name were a follower of St Paul and, in contrast, the infamous Titus Oates, an English conspirator and perjurer in the 17th century. It is probably best known today as the name of the hero of Mervyn Peake's *Gormenghast* books.

Toby *m.*
Toby is the English form of the Greek **Tobias**, itself derived from the Hebrew name which means 'the Lord is good'. The story of *Tobias and the Angel*, which is told in the Apocrypha was a favourite one in the Middle Ages. Punch's dog Toby is named after the dog that accompanied Tobias on his travels.

Tod, Todd *m.*
Originally a surname meaning 'fox', which has now come to be used as a first name.

Toinette see **Anthony**

Tom, Tommy see **Thomas**

Toni, Tony see **Anthony**

Tonya see **Antonia, Tanya**

Torcall see **Torquil**

Toria see **Victoria**

Tormod see **Norman**

Torquil *m.*
This is the English rendering of the Norse name, Thorketill ('Thor's cauldron). The first element is the name of the Norse thunder god, Thor. The original became *Torcall* in Gaelic, which was anglicized into Torquil. It is used in Scotland, especially in the Outer Hebrides and among the Macleod family, and it has occasionally been given in England.

Totty see **Charlotte**

Tracy *f. and m.*
This popular girl's name seems to have started life

as a pet form of **Teresa**. It is also found as *Tracey* and *Tracie*. Its beginnings as an independent name were probably helped by the use of the surname Tracy (from a French placename) as a boy's name, particularly as at the time when it first became popular Spencer Tracy (1900-67) was a well-known film star. However, its use for boys is now rare.

Travis *m.*
A surname used as a first name. It comes from the French word *traverser*, meaning 'to cross' and would have been given originally to a toll-collector.

Trevor *m.*
From the Welsh *Trefor*, meaning 'great homestead'. Trevor is the English spelling. *Trev* is the short form.

Tricia *see* Patricia

Triss *see* Beatrice

Tristan, Tristram *m.*
This is a name of obscure origin, possibly Pictish. It appears as the name of the noble hero of the medieval love stories of Tristram and **Isolda**.

When Tristram is escorting Isolda to be married to his uncle they drink a magic love-potion intended for the newly-weds by mistake, and are doomed to adulterous love until their tragic deaths. *Tristran* is also found.

Trixie *see* Beatrice

Troy *m.*
Troy was the ancient city in Asia Minor besieged by the Greeks for ten years . Its use as a first name was boosted in the 1960s by the actor Troy Donahue. It has been popular in Australia.

Trudi, Trudie, Trudy *see* Gertrude

Tudor, Tudur *see* Theodore

Turlough *see* Terence

Tyrone *m.*
The name of the Irish county, which means 'Eoghan's land', used as a first name. It was used in the past by the actor, Tyrone Power (1913-58) in the USA and by the British theatre director, Sir Tyrone Guthrie (1900-71). *Ty* is the short form, although Guthrie was known to his friends as Tony.

U

Ulick *see* **Ulysses, William**

Ulysses *m.*

This is the Latin name for the Greek hero
Odysseus, whose tale is told in Homer's *Odyssey*.
Though little used in England, Scotland or Wales,
it has been used in Ireland as an equivalent for
Ulick, an Irish form of **William**. James Joyce's
most famous novel bears this name.

Una *f.*

The etymology of this ancient Irish name is
obscure. It is also found in the forms *Oonagh* or
Oona (pronounced 'oo-na'), both of which are
also found in Scotland. *Juno*, influenced by the
name of the Roman queen of the gods, is another
Irish form, best known from Sean O'Casey's play
Juno and the Paycock (1924). The Elizabethan poet,
Edmund Spenser, took the Irish name Una and

gave it its Latin sense, 'one, unity', in his epic poem *The Faerie Queene*.

Unice *see* Eunice

Unity *f.*
This is one of the abstract virtue names that became quite common among Puritans after the Reformation. It is only rarely found today.

Ursula *f.*
From the Latin meaning 'little she-bear'. The name was fairly common in the Middle Ages on account of St Ursula, a 5th-century Cornish princess who, along with her companions, was murdered near Cologne while on pilgrimage. The name had a revival after Mrs Craik chose it for her heroine in her popular novel, *John Halifax, Gentleman* (1856).

V

Val *see* **Perceval, Valentine, Valerie**

Valentine *m. and. f.*

From the Latin *valens*, meaning 'strong' or 'healthy'. St Valentine was a 3rd-century Roman priest whose martyrdom happened to fall on February 14th, the eve of the celebrations of the pagan goddess Juno, when lots were drawn to choose lovers. The feast was absorbed into the Christian calendar and the name has been used in Britain since the 13th century. It can be used for either sex. *Valentina* is an alternative girl's form. *Val* is a common diminutive, shared with **Valerie**.

Valerie *f.*

This is the French form of the Roman family name *Valeria*, and was taken into use in Britain in the late 19th century. It comes from a word meaning 'to be in good health'. It has the short form *Val*.

Vanda *see* **Wanda**

Vanessa *f.*
This name was invented in the early 18th century by the author Jonathan Swift as a pet name for **Esther** Vanhomrigh. He took the first syllable of her surname and added Essa, which was probably a pet form of Esther.

Vaughn, Vaughan *m.*
From the Welsh *fychan*, meaning 'small one'.

Velma *f.*
A name of unknown origin, which came into use in the 1880s in the United States.

Venetia *f.*
The Latin name for the Italian city of Venice, used as a first name. In the past the name was thought to have some connection with **Venus**, the Roman goddess of love, which is very occasionally used as a first name.

Vera *f.*
This name has two possible derivations. One possible source is the Russian for 'faith', another is the Latin meaning 'true'. It was used in English

literature in the 19th century, and became popular in Britain at the beginning of the 20th. It is sometimes used as an abbreviation of **Veronica** (see also **Verena**).

Verena *f.*

The name of a rather obscure 3rd-century saint. Its meaning is not known, but may well come from the same source as **Vera**. St Verena lived in Switzerland and her name is popular there, but uses among English speakers probably owe something to the name being prominent in Henry James's novel *The Bostonians*.

Vergil *see* Virgil

Verity *f.*

From the old English word for 'truth'. It was first used by the Puritans in the 17th century, and has been quite common ever since. The variant, **Verily** ('truly'), is also found occasionally.

Vernon *m.*

Richard de Vernon was one of the companions of William the Conqueror. The surname comes from a French placename which means 'alder grove'. It was not used as a first name until the 19th century, when many such aristocratic names were taken into general use.

Veronica *f.*

Traditionally, this name is understood to derive from the Latin *vera icon*, meaning 'a true image'. St Veronica wiped the sweat from Christ's face when he was on his way to be crucified. A 'true image' of Christ's face was supposed to have appeared on the cloth she used. It is more likely, however, that the name is probably a form of **Berenice**. **Véronique** has long been popular in France, and it was from here that the name reached Scotland in the late 17th century. It does not appear much in England before the late 19th century (see also **Vera**).

Veva *see* Genevieve

Vic *see* Victor

Vickie, Vicky, Vikki *see* Victoria

Victor *m.*

This is the Latin for 'conqueror'. Although it occurs in medieval England it was not common until the 19th century when it was used as a boy's form of **Victoria**. The commonest short form is *Vic*.

Victoria *f.*

From the Latin for 'victory'. This name was hardly used in this country until the reign of Queen Victoria, who was named after her German mother. In the recent past the name has been very popular and is often found in one of its short forms, *Vicky*, *Vickie*, *Vikki* and *Toria*. *Vita* and *Viti* and the nickname **Queenie** are also found.

Vida *see* **Davida**

Vilma *see* **William**

Vina *see* **Davida**

Vincent *m.*

From the Latin meaning 'conquering'. There was a 3rd-century Spanish martyr of this name and the name occurs in English records from the 13th century. However, it was the 17th-century St Vincent de Paul who popularised the name when founded the Vincentian Order of the Sisters of Charity. The name became quite common in the 19th century. Its usual short form is *Vince*.

Viola, Violet *f.*

Viola is Latin for 'violet'. Although it does occur in

the Middle Ages, the modern use of this name is
due to Shakespeare, who gave it to the heroine of
Twelfth Night. **Violette** and **Violetta** have also been
used.

Virgil *m.*

The name of the great Roman poet. The original
spelling of his name was **Vergil**. The name has
been more used in the USA than in this country.

Virginia *f.*

Although there was a Roman family called
Virginus, the modern use of this name dates only
from 1587. Sir Walter Raleigh had called his newly
founded colony in North America Virginia, after
Elizabeth I, the 'Virgin Queen', and the name
Virginia was given to the first child born to the
settlers there. **Ginny**, **Gini** or **Jinny** is a common
pet form.

Vita, Viti *see* Victoria

Vitus *see* Guy

Vivian, Vivien *m. and f.*

From the Latin *vivianus*, which means 'lively'.
Vivian is now used for both sexes, but was
originally the masculine form, with Vivien, **Vivyan**

or *Vyvyan* mostly used for girls. The French *Vivienne* is always female. *Viv* is used for short.

Vonda *see* **Wanda**

Vyvyan *see* **Vivian**

W

Wal, Wally *see* **Wallace, Walter**

Wallace *m.*

From the surname of Sir William Wallace, the great Scottish patriot of the 13th century. The use of his surname as a first name started about a hundred years ago. The surname comes from the same root that gives us the word 'Welsh', but which was once used of the British in the North as well. Another spelling of the name is *Wallis*, found in North America where it is used for both sexes. The short forms, *Wal* and *Wally*, are shared with **Walter**.

Walter *m.*

From the Old German *Waldhar*, meaning 'army ruler'. The name was very popular among the Normans, and the name quickly became established in England. Sir Walter Raleigh is a well-known later example and he used the short form, *Wat*, for his son. *Walt*, *Wal* and *Wally* are more popular short forms in use today, and Walt is used as an independent name in North America.

Wanda *f.*
This is a Polish girl's name, probably connected with the word 'vandal'. Its use in this country possibly started when a novel of the name by Ouida was published in 1883. *Vanda* and *Vonda* are variants.

Warren *m.*
From the surname, which can either be from an old German tribe name, *Varin*, or from a Norman placename meaning 'a game-reserve'. The Normans introduced the forms Warin and Guarin to England and these led to the surnames Warren, Waring and Garnet.

Warwick *m.*
The name of the English town which means 'houses by the weir', used as a surname and then as a first name. *Warrie* is a pet form.

Wat *see* Walter

Wayne *m.*

This is a surname meaning 'cart' or 'cart-maker'.
Its use as a first name is mainly due to the
popularity of the actor John Wayne (1907-79).

Wendy *f.*

This name was first used by James Barrie in *Peter
Pan* (1904). The name started as 'Friendy-Wendy,'
a pet name for Barrie used by a child friend of his,
Margaret Henley. *Wenda* has been described as a
variant of Wendy, but is more probably a form of
Gwenda (see **Gwen**).

Wenonah *see* **Winona**

Wesley *m.*

John and Charles Wesley were the founders of
Methodism, and the name came to be used as a
first name in their honour. As a surname it means
'west meadow'. *Wes* is a short form.

Whitney *m. and f.*

This name, made famous by the singer Whitney
Houston, was originally a surname meaning
'(living) at the white island'. Its use as a first name
in the USA may owe something to its being the
surname of a wealthy family prominent in the

politics and arts of the country, and of Josiah Dwight Whitney (1819-96), geologist and surveyor, after whom Mount Whitney in South California, the highest mountain in the USA, is named.

Wilbur *m.*
This name is used in North America but is practically unknown in Britain. The most famous example was Wilbur Wright, who, with his brother **Orville**, made the first successful powered flight in 1903.

Wilfred, Wilfrid *m.*
From the Old English *Wilfrith*, meaning 'desiring peace'. St Wilfrid was an important figure in the 7th century, and his name was particularly popular in Yorkshire where he preached and founded the bishoprics of Ripon and Hexham. The name did not survive the Norman Conquest but was revived by high-church Anglicans in the 19th century. It has the pet form *Wilf*.

William, Wilma *m.*
From the Old German, meaning 'desiring protection'. William was always a popular name with the Normans, who brought it to England,

and, until the 13th century when it was ousted by John, it was the commonest of all names in England. *Will* or *Willie* are the old short forms but *Bill* and **Billie** are more usual today. *Gwilym,* shortened to *Gwill,* is the Welsh form of the name, and *Liam* a short form which has spread from Ireland; *Ulick* is another Irish form. Feminine forms which have been used occasionally are *Wilhelmina* and *Wilma*. Their pet forms include *Willa* or *Vilma, Minnie* and *Minna* and *Elma* (see **Elmer**). These feminine forms are more popular in America where German immigrants have spread their use.

Winifred *f.*

From the Welsh feminine name *Gwenfrewi,* anglicized as Winifred and later confused with the Old English male name *Winfrith,* meaning 'friend of peace'. St Winifred, a 7th-century saint, is said to have been decapitated by a Welsh prince when she rejected his advances, but then was restored miraculously to life. Although she was a popular saint in the Middle Ages, her name was not used much until the 16th century. It was a very popular name at the turn of the century. *Win, Winnie* and less often *Freda*, are short forms. *Winifrid* is also used.

Winona *f.*

This is a Sioux word meaning 'eldest daughter'. It is also the name of a city in Minnesota. The name occurs as **Wenonah** in Longfellow's poem *Hiawatha* (1855), and can also be found as **Wynona**.

Winston *m.*

This is the name of a small village in Gloucestershire, which became a surname. The name has been used in the Churchill family since 1620, when Sir Winston Churchill, father of the 1st Duke of Marlborough, was born. His mother was Sarah Winston. It has come into use in honour of a more recent Sir Winston Churchill (1874-1965) to mark his contribution to world affairs.

Wyn, Wynfor, Wynne *see* Gwyn

Wynona *see* Winona

X

Xan, Xander *see* **Alexander**

Xanthe *f.*
From the Greek meaning 'yellow'. It has occasionally been used in Britain.

Xara *see* **Zara**

Xavier *m.*
The surname of St Francis Xavier (1506-52) used as a first name. It is occasionally spelt *Zavier* and there are rare feminine forms, *Xavia*, *Zavia*, *Xaviera* and *Xaverine*.

Xenia *f.*
The Greek word for 'hospitality'. It is only occasionally found see also **Zena**).

Y

Yasmin, Yasmina, Yasmine *see* **Jasmine**

Yehudi *see* **Jude**

Yolanda *f.*
From the Greek meaning 'violet flower'. The Gilbert and Sullivan opera *Iolanthe* comes from the same root. *Yolande* is the French form.

Yorick *m.*
This name is most famous from its use by Shakespeare in his play, *Hamlet*. It probably derives from a phonetic form of the Danish *Georg* (pronounced 'Yeorg'). It has only rarely been used as a given name.

Ysabel *see* **Isabel**

Yseult(e), Ysolde *see* **Isolda**

Yves *see* **Ivo, Ivor, Yvonne**

Yvonne, Yvette *f.*
These are French names meaning 'yew'. They are
female pet forms of the Breton boy's name, *Yves*.
The boy's name has never been common in
Britain, but the girl's versions are quite popular.

Z

Zachary *m.*
The English form of *Zacharias*, the Greek for the Hebrew *Zachariah* or *Zechariah*, meaning 'the Lord has remembered'. Zachary was used occasionally in the Middle Ages, but did not become at all common until the Puritans adopted it in the 17th century. They took it to America where it has recently become popular, together with the short form *Zak* or *Zack*. It is now spreading to this country. *Zacchaeus* and *Zakki* are other forms of the name.

Zak *see* **Zachary, Isaac**

Zakki *see* **Zachary**

Zandra *see* **Sandra**

Zara *f.*
This is said to be an Arabic name meaning

'brightness, splendour of dawn'. It has a long history of literary use, but came to the attention of the general public in 1981 when Princess Anne, the Princess Royal used it as her daughter's name. It is occasionally found as *Xara*.

Zavia, Zavier *see* Xavier

Zeb *m.*

This can be a short form of such Hebrew names as *Zebulun* ('exaltation') or *Zebedee* ('my gift'), or can simply be an attempt by parents to find an unusual name. Similarly *Zed* can be seen as a short form of *Zedekiah* ('justice of the Lord').

Zechariah *see* Zachary

Zed, Zedekiah *see* Zeb

Zeke *see* Ezekiel

Zelda *see* Griselda

Zena *f.*

One theory is that this name comes from a Persian word meaning 'woman'. Another makes it a pet form of various other names such as *Zinaida* which comes from 'Zeus', the Greek king of the

377

gods, the name of two Russian saints; and another a variation of **Xenia**. It is also found as *Zina*.

Zenobia *f.*
This was the name of a great Queen of Palmyra (modern Syria) in the 3rd century AD. She was seen as a threat to the Eastern Roman Empire, and her aggressive foreign policy forced the Emperor Aurelian to invade. This he did successfully and put an end to her power, though he spared her life. The name appears in Cornwall from the 16th century but the reason for this is unknown.

Zillah *f.*
From the Hebrew for 'shade'. The name occurs in the Old Testament (Genesis IV, 19-23) and was used occasionally after the Reformation.

Zina, Zinaida *see* Zena

Zita *f.*
This was the name of the last Empress of Austria, who although deposed shortly after the end of the First World War, only died in 1989. It comes from an Italian word for 'little girl' and was the name of

a humble but good maid who became the patron saint of domestic servants.

Zoe, Zoë *f.*

This is the Greek word for 'life'. The Alexandrian Jews used it to translate the Hebrew equivalent for **Eve** into Greek. The name spread throughout the Eastern Church but has only been used in Britain in the last hundred years.

Zola *f.*

The name of the French novelist, Emile Zola (1840-1902,) used as a first name. Although best known from the runner, Zola Budd, the name has been used before. The lead singer of the 1950s pop group *The Platters* was Zola Taylor.

Zuleika *f.*

From the Persian meaning 'brilliant beauty'. The name is known from Max Beerbohm's satirical novel *Zuleika Dobson* (1911), whose heroine is so beautiful that all the young men at Oxford University kill themselves for love of her.

Most popular girls' and boys' names

The following lists show the most popular names featuring in the birth announcements column of *The Independent* newspaper during a recent eighteen-month period. Spellings show the most popular form of the name.

Girls

First names		*Second names*	
1	Emily	1	Elizabeth
2	Alice	2	Rose
	Isabel	3	Mary
4	Sophie	4	Louise
5	Eleanor	5	Clare
	Katharine	6	Anne
7	Elizabeth	7	Victoria
	Emma	8	Jane
	Rachel	9	Charlotte
10	Lucy	10	Sarah
11	Charlotte	11	Alice
	Rebecca	12	Emily
13	Olivia	13	May
14	Hannah	14	Grace
	Jessica	15	Kate
			Rachel

Other popular girls' names include Alexandra, Amy, Chloe, Georgina, Katie, Laura, Lauren, and Samantha.

Boys

	First names		*Second names*
1	Thomas	1	James
2	James	2	William
3	Alexander	3	John
4	William	4	Alexander
5	Benjamin	5	Edward
	Edward	6	Charles
7	Oliver	7	David
8	Samuel	8	Henry
9	Henry	9	Michael
10	Matthew	10	Robert
11	Charles	11	George
12	George	12	Thomas
	Christopher		Peter
14	Jack	14	Christopher
15	Jonathan	15	Richard

Other popular boys' names include Adam, Daniel, Harry, and Jamie.

COLLINS GEM

Bestselling Collins Gem titles include:

Gem English Dictionary (£3.50)
Gem Calorie Counter (£2.99)
Gem Thesaurus (£2.99)
Gem French Dictionary (£3.50)
Gem German Dictionary (£3.50)
Gem Basic Facts Mathematics (£2.99)
Gem Birds (£3.50)
Gem Wild Flowers (£3.50)
Gem Card Games (£3.50)
Gem World Atlas (£3.50)

All Collins Gems are available from your local bookseller or can be ordered direct from the publishers.

In the UK, contact Mail Order, Dept 2M, HarperCollins Publishers, Westerhill Rd, Bishopbriggs, Glasgow, G64 2QT, listing the titles required and enclosing a cheque or p.o. for the value of the books plus £1.00 for the first title and 25p for each additional title to cover p&p. Access and Visa cardholders can order on 041-772 2281 (24 hr).

In Australia, contact Customer Services, HarperCollins Distribution, Yarrawa Rd, Moss Vale 2577 (tel. [048] 68 0300). **In New Zealand**, contact Customer Services, HarperCollins Publishers, 31 View Rd, Glenfield, Auckland 10 (tel. [09] 444 3740). **In Canada**, contact your local bookshop.

All prices quoted are correct at time of going to press.

COLLINS GEM

Other Gem titles that may interest you include:

Gem Travel Games
An indispensable help in keeping children amused on journeys   **£3.50**

Gem Basic Facts Physics, Chemistry, Biology, Mathematics and Computers
A range of illustrated dictionaries in key school subjects. Each book explains the essential terms and concepts in each subject and so is invaluable for exam revision   **£2.99 each**

Gem World Atlas
The ideal quick-reference atlas, fully updated to show the new political boundaries of Eastern Europe   **£3.50**

Gem Human Body
A compact and fully illustrated manual to the human body: how it works, keeping it healthy and possible problems   **£3.50**

Gem First Aid
A fully illustrated, handy-sized guide to the essential first aid techniques for both major and minor injuries   **£3.50**